D0096172

F

B

Cover image   "Clock, Deck, and Movement"
(performed in San Francisco, December 2007)

Photo by   Cynthia Sailers

Cover design by   Rita Lascaro
Book design by   Rebecca Wolff

Published in the United States by   Fence Books
Science Library 320
University at Albany
1400 Washington Avenue
Albany, NY 12222
www.fenceportal.org

Fence Books are distributed by   University Press of New England
www.upne.com

and printed in Canada by   Westcan Printing Group
www.westcanpg.com

Library of Congress Cataloguing in Publication Data
    Toscano, Rodrigo [1964–]
    Collapsible Poetics Theater/Rodrigo Toscano

Library of Congress Control Number: 2008934252

ISBN 1-934200-18-2
ISBN 13: 978-1-934200-18-6

FIRST EDITION

The National Poetry Series was established in 1978 to ensure the publication of five poetry books annually through five participating publishers. Publication is funded by the Lannan Foundation; Stephen Graham; Joyce & Seward Johnson Foundation; Glenn and Renee Schaeffer, Juliet Lea Hillman Simonds Foundation; Tiny Tiger Foundation; and, Charles B. Wright III.

2007 Competition Winners

Joe Bonomo of DeKalb, Illinois
Installations
Chosen by Naomi Shihab Nye for Penguin Books

Oni Buchanan of Brighton, Massachusetts
Spring
Chosen by Mark Doty for University of Illinois Press

Sabra Loomis of New York, New York
House Held Together by Winds
Chosen by James Tate for HarperCollins Publishers

Donna Stonecipher of Berlin, Germany
The Cosmopolitan
Chosen by John Yau for Coffee House Press

Rodrigo Toscano of Brooklyn, New York
Collapsible Poetics Theater
Chosen by Marjorie Welish for Fence Books

COLLAPSIBLE POETICS THEATER

Rodrigo Toscano

COLLAPSIBLE POETICS THEATER

Rodrigo Toscano

winner of the National Poetry Series
selected by Marjorie Welish

Albany, New York

ACKNOWLEDGEMENTS

Some of these scores have appeared in the following periodicals and anthologies: *Ecopoetics, Jubilat, Can't Exist, With + Stand, West Coast Line, Cross Cultural Poetics (XCP), Slightly West, Capilano Review, President's Choice, Brooklyn Rail, Filling Station, Plantarchy, WinteRed, 88 A Journal of Contemporary Poetry, New Ohio Review, Jacket, Sibila, Respiro, Nypoesi, Coconut, Junta, War & Peace, Ceptuetics, Eleven Eleven, Specs, Fascicle, Mark's Zine, Coconut, Jacket, Boxon, Plantarchy, Respiro, Diasporic Avant-Gardes.* The author wishes to thank the publishers for their support and encouragement.

Collapsible Poetics Theater (CPT) would not be possible without the tremendous generosity, talents, and energy from the following people: *Tom Orange, John Beer, Leonard Schwartz, Kristin Prevallet, M. Magnus, David Brazil, Lorraine Graham, Jason Conger, Laura Elrick, Holly Melgard, Balan Villanueva, Suzanne Stein, Alli Warren, Riva Roller, Anna Moschovakis, Tim Peterson, Brendan Lorber, Aaron Kiely, Urayoan Noel, Edwin Torres, Linda Russo, Mark Wallace, Mel Nichols, Brian Kim Stefans, Christian Bok, Brent Cunningham, Dan Fisher, Chuck Stebelton, Brenda Cardenas, Rob Halpern, Anselm Berrigan, Roberto Harrison, Anne Kingsbury, Jeremy Gardner, Rod Smith, Jocelyn Saidenberg, Melissa Christine Goodrum, Emily Crocker, Clare Alexa Sammons, Lil Luce, Gregory Stuart, Cole Swensen, Kelly Brown, Frank Sherlock, Kaplan Harris, Michael Barron, Filip Marinovitch, Kish Songbear, Lindsey Boldt, Dennis Somera, Erika Staiti, CA Conrad, Alicia Askenase, Carla Harryman, Steve Benson, Lytle Shaw, Deborah Meadows, Nicholas Perrin, Andrea Actis, Donato Mancini, Margot Butler, Mariner Janes, Nikki Reimer, Paolo Javier, Katie Leo-Keast, Sha Cage, Robert St. Clair, Gregory Houser, Claire Hanson, Sophie Gordon, Brian King, Camila Martin, Sally Zebrick, Teela Royset, Fawn Wilderson-Legros, Sha Cage, Katie Leo-Keast, Jacob Knabb, Melissa Severin, Linda Russo, Josh Corey, Fred Sasaki, David Kirschenbaum, Jonathan Skinner, Cori Copp, Nora Griffin, David Michael Wolach,* and *Elizabeth Williamson.*

Special thanks to Maxwell Heller and Stephanie Young for their keen artistic insight, coordinating prowess, and steadfast friendship throughout this journey.

Also, my deepest gratitude to my co-workers at the Labor Institute (Les Leopold, Paul Renner, Sally Silvers, Jim Young, Joe Anderson, Jean Urano, and Kathy Burris), whose tacit material, political, and personal support for this project so exemplifies the spirit of institute founder Tony Mazzocchi (1926-2002), "Movements grow in desperate times. We are being born."

CPT performance pics can be found at: http://poeticstheater. typepad.com/photos/rt_pics/index.html

CPT video excerpts can be found at: http://cpt.blip.tv

Contents

TRUAX INIMICAL

A TRANS-MODERN MASQUE FOR FOUR VOICES

BEAST HATH MADE US, BEAST HATH NOT

PART 1

•

Don't tread on you? Entity. Of the expansive accumulative. Society. Inalienable? Dsynchronous. Siempre. Torn up and tearing. Sacred and profane. Silly and sublime. Ascendant. Techne. *Of what's oppositional, of what's not. Of what's recuperative, of what's not. Walking tall. Life and death. Power and grace. Alienable Dividuals. Entities. Seek a freedom* in, not *from. Alienable Dividual. Sees the diff, bears the brunt, speaks the sum. A sliver of your own self, striving.* Siempre.

(1) *Very* Lilliputian
(2) Adorable
(3) Snuggly
(4) Secretive

(2) Obsessive
(3) Frenetic
(1) Subversive
(4) Supplantive

(1) Somewhat impish
(2) Kind of frumpish
(3) A bit schmaltzy
(4) *Very* hammy

(1) Formal in comportment
(3) Rounded in interests
(4) Interested in roundness
(2) Square to the core

(4) Body-body-centric
(3) Touchy
(2) Bitchy
(1) Slaphappy

(3) A *real* scroller
(2) A *real* pointer
(1) A *real* clicker
(4) A *real* selector

(1) Scrolling
(4) Pointing
(2) Clicking
(3) Selecting

(1) Scrolling
(4) Pointing
(2) Clicking
(3) Selecting

(4) I was very disappointed by the doping up of red-hot scientific phenomenon into a consumerist cocktail

(1) Scrolling
(4) Pointing
(2) Clicking
(3) Selecting

(2) Repixilating an image of reality by way of titanium pellet manufacture and promo

(1) Scrolling
(4) Pointing
(2) Clicking
(3) Selecting

(4) Synchronizing connections with entities very similar to its own

(1) Scrolling
(4) Pointing
(2) Clicking
(3) Selecting

(2) Feeling deep that what is to be known ... is to be known

(1) Scrolling
(4) Pointing
(2) Clicking
(3) Selecting

(4) *Very* Lilliputian

(1) Circumscribing a zone of action for itself
(2) Designating specific entry-points for others
(3) Truly steroidal eager pregnant with evocative jettisonings of—
(4) A bit-bonding global demand for—

(1-4) *CULTURE!?*

(3) Culture
(1) *Culture?*
(4) Retail
(2) Wholesale

(1) Scrolling
(4) Pointing
(2) Clicking
(3) Selecting

(1) What about "Rise Brazil!" (in quotes like that) ... *sans* affable you
(4) What about "Rise South Africa!" (in quotes like that) ... *sans* affable you
(2) What about "Rise India!" (in quotes like that) ... *sans* affable you
(3) What about "Rise Azerbaijan!" (in quotes like that) ... *sans* affable you

(4) *Sans* affable me
(3) *Sans* miserly me
(2) *Sans* miserable me
(1) *Sans* miserly miserable *pivotal* me

(1) A defoliated palm at the end of the Empire
(2) A coconut falls, rolls, and settles on the beach
(3) A coconut is cut out and replaced with a cannonball
(4) Cannonball coconut chocolate-covered cream

(1-4) MMMM!

(3) Man, this *sans* affable me thing's the thing!
(1) Thing about the thing is—
(4) It's . . . thingy
(2) Thingy?

(1-4) MMMM!

(1) Scrolling
(4) Pointing
(2) Clicking
(3) Selecting

(3) How will I *ever* find my way back to Kansas?
(4) By way of Bombay of course
(1) On a horse on the pampas of Argentina
(2) Put out to pasture: knowledge, skill, experience

(1) An entire nation cut out and replaced with a less productive animal
(3) Are you that horse?
(2) A horse cut out and replaced with a less porous national border
(4) Are you that donkey?

(1) I was—am about ready to get—not only *very* FRIGHTENED
(3) I've heard that one before
(2) Me too
(4) Me too

(1) But *very* disappointed by the lack of any stated counter-capitalistic
(4) As how to get from Mendoza to Walla Walla
(3) By way of Marx to Marti
(2) Am I that mule?

(3) People getting what they want how they want when they want it
(2) People getting fumbly stumbly crazy with it
(4) People getting stuck there
(1) People getting theoretical about it too

(2) Like in ancient Egypt?
(4) Like the near complete opposite!

4

(1) Tribeca?
(3) Topeka!

(4) At the core of the Empire is an authentic voice that sounds like a controlling sleazy son of a—
(3) You mean dragonfly?
(1) By entomologist's projection only
(2) Lightheaded, I'm getting lightheaded

(1) Supplantive
(3) Subventing more like
(4) Supra-Convect-
(2) When is this thing gonna get *selectively* violent toward

(1) The more arch-romantic the better by god!
(2) The more textured the proclamation the healthier the tendons
(3) The more exposed the curve of the neck the less modernistic?
(4) The more entrenched the relativism the more institutional uptake?

(1) To repetition!
(4) To variation!
(3) What else?
(2) *Assonance*

(1) Scrolling
(4) Pointing
(2) Clicking
(3) Selecting

(1) I am very heartened by the extension of architectural thought into poetic discourse
(4) I am very heartened by the extension of computer speak into poetic discourse
(2) I am very heartened by the extension of bio-tech talk into poetic discourse
(3) I am very heartened by the extension of neo-pop art-think into poetic discourse

(2) I am not so *thrilled-to-the-bone* walking through downtown Paterson
(3) I am not so *thrilled-to-the-bone* with my index finger locking up
(4) I am not so *thrilled-to-the-bone* with those mickies making you such

the dragonfly
(1) I am not so *thrilled-to-the-bone* by that text's play-by-play

(1) I suppose . . . I am rather burdened . . . by the premature truncation of
poetic discourse unto social discourse in general
(3) I've heard that one before
(2) Me too
(4) Me too

(4) At the edge of the Empire is a synthetic voice that sounds like a
recorded loop with emotional highlighting tweaked-in later
(3) You mean you
(2) By copping, *only* me
(1) Jittery, I'm getting jittery

(2) *Very* Lilliputian

(1) Scrolling
(4) Pointing
(2) Clicking
(3) Selecting

(1) What about "put the big shinola on the high priest of English syntax" (in
quotes like that) . . . *sans* (in brackets) [*integral*] you
(3) What about "shit-on-a-cracker realism, express line 1" (in quotes like
that) . . . *sans* (in brackets) [*integral*] you
(2) What about "shamanistic shalackings, transnational" (in quotes like
that) . . . *sans* (in brackets) [*integral*] you
(4) What about "shell-game avantist cultural market slice" (in quotes like
that) . . . *sans* (in brackets) [*integral*] you

(3) *Assonance*
(4) On the line I'm putting it
(2) A bit above it I am hovering
(1) A bit below it—me—sly (maybe)

(1) Scrolling
(4) Pointing
(2) Clicking
(3) Selecting

(1) A refurbished laptop in a crate in the Indian Ocean
(2) A wave-swell five stories high approaching
(3) A decision to bare leeward 45 degrees
(4) A good decision, in the end, MS Word working well enough on 500 MHz / 64MB Ram, 120 U.S. dollars + no charge (ground-rate) shipping

(2) Your weapon of choice . . . U.S. dollars?
(3) Avec me
(1) Avec ministerial me
(4) Avec ministerial beaucoup flappable me

(3) *Bold* conception that of Marti's—why not refurbish it?
(1) *Bold* conception that of DuBois's—why not ship it?
(4) *Bold* conception that of Sub-Commandante's—why not wholesale it?
(2) *Bold* conception that of Chavez's—why not retail it?

(4) We've got two pots brewing in the back . . .
(3) One of them's good for you . . .
(2) One of them's not . . .
(1) We'll decide which one you get . . .

(1-4) WHEN YOU GET HERE!

(2) *Very* Lilliputian

(1) I am not a little discomfited by the employment of such overtly finance-capitalist lexicons subventing a class-antagonistic conceptual work of art

(4) Scrolling—by which it pans for values

(2) Pointing—by which it recognizes antagonism

(3) Clicking—by which it relieves momentary tension

(4) Selecting is predicated on social psychologies that are themselves predicated on recognized values in contention?

(2) *Very* Lilliputian

7

(3) People giving what they give when they give how they give it
(2) People giving all they've got—zip
(4) People sucking wind—in sensuous postures
(1) People trying to get centered in every possible way

(2) A deranged donkey in Dhahran, discoing
(3) A sullen mule in America, meditating
(4) A horse on the pampas of Argentina, nostrils flaring
(1) Glue Factory Press publishes works of exceptional quality, works that "explore" "spaces" "between" "spaces" "between" "spaces"

(2) The more affectatious the text the *less*
(1) The less intrepid the lexicon the *more*
(3) The more indulgent the audience the *less*
(4) The less animalistic the actor the *more*

(1) Ammunition!
(3) Propaganda!
(4) What else?
(2) Innocence!

(4) Man, maybe we should just learn Arabic, *sans* all this
(1) Man, maybe we should just pick wild crabapples, and call it a day
(3) Man, maybe we should just start a small pottery business
(2) Man, maybe we should just accrue a sense of generic indignation and see what happens

(1) When the wall fell
(2) Oh boy, here we go!
(3) When the wall fell
(4) You had an epiphany about your *own* repression, but not anyone else's?

(1) What also fell was the sense of a grand project gone awry
(2) "Awry" *molted* into Absolutist Rejectionism
(3) Which *molted* into Absolutist Affirmation of its opposite
(4) An invisible, ubiquitous wall, a suck-bot, bit-bonding global demand for—

(1-4) *CULTURE!?*

8

(3) Cope, I feel I should just cope
(2) Is that the byword of the Modern American Worker?
(4) Seize the towers of Law! Custom! Manners!
(1) Off with thine baby-faces of ecstasy, *sans* death, waving its sickle

(4) In the basement of the Empire is a two-year-old who'll grow up to denounce her keeper's accomodationism
(3) Is this what they call *realpolitik?*
(1) Wabbit hunting season!
(2) Wabbit, the *un*duck

(1) I scrimp
(2) You scrimp
(3) We all scrimp
(4) For less managerial consciousness in poetic discourse

END OF PART 1

TRUAX INIMICAL

PART 2

•

(1·2) I
(3·4) Fly
(1·2) In
(3·4) The
(1·2) Deep
(3·4) Of
(1·2) The
(3·4) Night

(1·2) I
(3·4) Fly
(1·2) Toward
(3·4) The
(1·2) Source
(3·4) Of
(1·2) The
(3·4) Light

(1) Wings

(4) Flutter flutter flutter

(2) Moon

(3) Sends down her light

(1) The lily is lovely to see

(4) The fennel and the mandrake

(3) Horses here stamp joyously

(1·2) We

(3-4) Fly
(1-2) Toward
(3-4) The
(1-2) Face
(3-4) Of
(1-2) The
(3-4) Moon

(1-2) We
(3-4) Drink
(1-2) Deep
(3-4) Of
(1-2) The
(3-4) Light
(1-2) Come
(3-4) Down

(1-2) We
(3-4) Seek
(1-2) New
(3-4) Soils
(1-2) For
(3-4) Our
(1-2) *Own*
(3-4) Growth

(1) Skidding over the brackish waters

(4) Sunlight glinting in the ruddy eastern sky

(2) The towers of midtown sparkling in their resplendent monotony

(3) The heliports busy busy busy

(1-2) We
(3-4) Dig
(1-2) Deep
(3-4) Toward
(1-2) The
(3-4) Roots
(1-2) Of
(3-4) Selves

(1) Slots into milliseconds, for feelings

(3) Evaporative nervous density

(2) Fog & fog's taste in the mouth

(1·2) We
(3·4) Lay
(1·2) Breaths
(3·4) In
(1·2) Short
(3·4) Rows—
(1·2) To
(3·4) Sprout

(4) Angle up, steady

(3) Lift off

(2) Flutter flutter

(1) Over the rock where so many beings come to float upon its shores, so many lively deadly beings, glowing and glowing out, each unto the other—

(3) Spectral

(4) Inimical quotient

(2) Conditioning

(1·2) We
(3·4) Fight
(1·2) Hard
(3·4) For
(1·2) Time
(3·4) Off
(1·2) To
(3·4) Think

(1-2) We
(3-4) Time
(1-2) These
(3-4) Small
(1-2) Words
(3-4) To
(1-2) Those
(3-4) Thoughts

(1-2) We
(3-4) Think
(1-2) To
(3-4) Act
(1-2) On
(3-4) Our
(1-2) *Own*
(3-4) Wits

(4) Speech, of an epoch past, function of a harried now, detourned
rabid mess of a mind called up just in time for the devout
devouring of some

(3) Stutter

(2) Cul-

(1) Flutter

(4) -ture

(1-2) We
(3-4) Plot
(1-2) In
(3-4) The
(1-2) Thick
(3-4) Of
(1-2) The
(3-4) Night

(1-2) We
(3-4) Land

(1-2) Soft
(3-4) On
(1-2) A
(3-4) Frond's
(1-2) Long
(3-4) Stem

(1-2) We
(3-4) Sip
(1-2) Dew
(3-4) From
(1-2) Our
(3-4) Sense
(1-2) Of
(3-4) Past

(1-2) They
(3-4) Dash
(1-2) Mad
(3-4) Towards
(1-2) The
(3-4) Cliff's
(1-2) Steep
(3-4) Ledge

(1) Cappy, Schleppy

(4) Schleppy, Cappy

(2) What's a Cappy got to do with it?

(3) What's a Schleppy got to do with it?

(1) When's a Cappy come?

(4) When's a Schleppy go?

(2) When's a Schleppy come?

(3) When's a Cappy go?

(1) Con·
(2) di·
(1) tion·
(2) ing

(3) Dis·
(4) tor·
(3) tion·
(4) ist

(1) Ab·
(2) so·
(1) lute·
(2) ist

(3) Blind·
(4) side·
(3) ed·
(4) ness

(3) Con·
(4) di·
(3) tion·
(4) ing

(1) Dis·
(2) tor·
(1) tion·
(2) ist

(3) Ab·
(4) so·
(3) lute·
(4) ist

(1) Blind·
(2) side·
(1) ed·
(2) ness

(2) And if you're
(3) You learn to
(2) Hell bent to
(3) Act on your
(2) Bust out
(3) Own wits

(2) And if you're
(3) You learn to
(2) Hell bent to
(3) Act on your
(2) Bust out
(3) Own wits

(1-4) Flutter, flutter

END OF PART 2

TRUAX INIMICAL

PART 3

•

(1) Life is *pulse* really
(3) And there's compression
(2) And there's decompression
(4) Panoramic but seen from within

(1) A tetrahedron from all sides
(4) Complex
(2) Beautiful
(3) Many-sided

(4) We once revered flat surfaces
(1) *¡No mas!*
(3) We once pronounced chance king
(2) *¡No mas!*

(1) How's it that we're four distinct entities here?
(4) How's it that we're singular and one-at-a-time?
(2) How's it that we're each one-quarter of one whole?
(3) How's it that we're each four times more than the other?

(4) Life is bluster too!
(1) *Movimiento Al Socialismo*
(3) Highlight it
(2) Copy it

(1-4)
HOLD YOUR
SCHEISSE
COUSIN!

TOES OFF
THE
KEYBOARD!

(3) How did a chunk of charcoal become a gem?
(4) By compression—*I told you*—life is bluster too
(2) Flies would have it otherwise
(1) Where do I sign?

(3) Evo Morales must *manifest*—not just paste it "Full Nationalization of Gas Deposits"
(1) Life is a constituent assembly in the making
(4) Life is a coca leaf for the taking
(2) Flies would have it otherwise

(3) *Moviemiento a la poesia translinguistica*
(1) Where do I sign?
(2) *Moviemiento a la poesia multimetricalista*
(4) Where do I sign?

(1) We once coveted interiorities of bohemian moms and pops
(2) *No mo'!*
(4) We once sported vertical-striped acrylic death-of-the-I sweaters—and twill pants
(3) *No mo'!*

(1) Sign here
(4) And here
(2) And here
(3) And here

(1) And here
(4) And here
(2) And here
(3) And here

(2) When does a line of verse become a chant?
(1) Damn I hate speech!
(4) I hate text
(3) I hate both your asses

(2) And here
(4) Have I told you about how a site-specific approach might have been a more efficient—
(1) *¡Moviemiento Al Compacto Transregional!*
(3) You did—and rather *inefficiently*

(2) How does a baby become a corpse?
(1) By too much autonomy ("don't tread on me")
(3) By not enough autonomy (volonté genéral)
(4) Damn I hate fudging the fundamental difference between Locke and Rousseau

(1) How's it that we're four distinct entities here?
(4) How's it that we're singular and one-at-a-time?
(2) How's it that we're each one-quarter of one whole?
(3) How's it that we're each four times more than the other?

(1)
Warm breeze from the South Pole
Flows towards the North Pole
Bends vernal pool grasses ·
Gently layering
These cold
Words
Bending

(3) Toes on the keyboard cousin—hit me.

(1)
Fresh milk from the sow-cow
Flows towards the kick bucket
Gladdens a gentle heart
Gently quenching
These parched
Words
Suckling

(2) Manifesting new trade pacts—based on social needs—say—
between—Venezuela, Brazil, Argentina, Cuba—possibly Ecuador
and Peru—and of course, now—Bolivia . . . can be a bulwark against
constraint-as-chance—World Bank—regional—*poetics*

(4) A tetrahedron from all sides
(2) Complex
(3) Beautiful
(1) Many-sided

(3) I found another penny on 14th street in Manhattan, tucked halfway between the chained door of a kiosk and the cold January pavement— early morning, and it looked pretty schmutzy this penny, and it was—yuk, but as it is my habit (ok, psychology), not to abandon congealed labor, and what's more—the ritual is to rub it to make out the date—and I always compare that date to another date, and think . . . how did I get here

(1) Life is *pulse* really
(3) And there's compression
(2) And there's decompression
(4) Panoramic but seen from within

(3) Bechtel—in Bolivia, tried (but failed) to make collecting rainwater illegal
(4) Life is bluster on the move—for sure
(2) *¡Movimiento a la construcción de bombas poeticas efectivas para explotar la dirección general de Bechtel!*
(1) Where do I sign up for a Spanish class?

(4) What *did* Bolívar think about Toussaint thinking about Robespierre?
(3) What did Robespierre think about Toussaint thinking about Rousseau?
(2) What did Frederick Douglass think about Toussaint thinking about Thomas Paine?
(1) On the senate floor, why did Senator Preston Brooks from the Palmetto State almost cane to death senator Charles Sumner from the Bay State—May 22, 1856?

(2) We once were intimidated by the words "vagrant" "fugitive" "illegal"
(3) We once were cowed by legalistic national literatures and/or positivist frameworks for spontaneous cultural expression
(1) We once were ashamed to declare complete independence from the three chunks of charcoal known as Canada, Mexico, and the U.S.
(4) We once were too timid to proclaim a more translucent gem

(3) Another penny I spotted on Bedford Avenue in Brooklyn, but on close inspection it was a one-cent euro (which can't buy you a sprig of Bulgarian rosemary) but there it was tucked underneath a Polish nanny's white boot—goodness—my time's *certainly* got to be more valuable than the 10 minute wait to retrieve it, but, as it is my praxis (ok, neurosis), not to abandon congealed labor, I poised myself for the moment—swooped

in, snatched it, rubbed it . . . compared the date to another date . . .
and thought . . . where the hell am I going

(1)
Trapped steam from the collection chamber
Shoots towards the escape valve
Sparks methane gasses
Rapidly setting
These copper-nickel
Turbines
A-turnin!

(2) Eyes on the energy exchange agreements cousins—¡a-hoowa!

(4)
Busybodies from the Peripheral Poetic Zone
Bore into the Central Poetic Zone
Flies, crickets, roaches
Steadily creeping
Toward these acid
Realities
Settling

(3) Heroically? To casts one's lot—again—with culture?
(1) Candelabra of exchange values, twitching hominoids glittering (I
mean . . . overhead)
(2) Life is manure, in' it?
(4) *And* crop

(1) Ruefully, as I will've slammed the door—on it
Though the door is missing
And that's hot lead on the dragonfly's eyes

(2) Determinatively, as I might've made the door—myself
But the materials are missing
And the know-how lacking

(3) Ironically, as I'm directing—conceptually—the *idea* of a door
Not driving a single nail myself
Who's listening anyway?

(4) Stoically, to casts one's lot—once more—with culture?
Culture—it's listening?
(I'm not)

(1) The sound of a door . . . closing . . . *where's that sound of a door closing dammit!*
(3) The shorts were $7.99 upon asking, so I gave her $8.00, and she said thank you with a finality that horrified my world-historical mission (ok, tic) not to "abandon congealed labor," and so I said (meekly) "I'm sorry, but it's for my—collection" . . . when instantly the price shot up to ten dollars—and zero cents; but after a protracted (and of course, dialectical) struggle, I managed to seize a $9.00—and one cent—*poetic*—pair of shorts

(1) Where do I sign up?
(2) What are you out of your freakin' mind!?
(3) *¡Moviemiento a la poesia trangresista materialista!*
(4) Flies even—have it otherwise

(1) Sign here
(4) And here
(2) And here
(3) And here

(4) We once were titillated by the phrases "free trade" "inhibition release" "attach ye not to the material things of this world"
(2) We once were titty-twizzled by delicious descriptions of perennially open-ended poetics and/or border crossing aesthetics *sans* actual bodies moving freely
(3) We once were too bashful to conceive and design and construct a tetrahedron from the conception of the translucent gem henceforward to be known as ESMERALDA
(1) We once were too repressed to take a nude collective bubble bath with ESMERALDA

(2) And here . . .
(1) What about here?
(3) And there
(4) Now—submit that to the assembly

(1) Me—as only me?
(4) Sort of
(2) Me—as only me?
(3) Kind of

(4) Me—as only me?
(1) Maybe
(3) Me—as only me?
(2) Close enough

(1) How's it that we're four hundred million distinct entities here?
(4) How's it that we're singular and one-at-a-time?
(2) How's it that we're each one four hundred millionth of one whole?
(3) How's it that we're each four hundred million times more than the other?

(2) Blake—advised Paine—to jet to France
(3) Robespierre—gave the nod—to Toussaint
(1) Douglas—became ambassador—to Haiti
(4) Du Bois—kicked a high volley—to Hughes—striker extraordinaire

(3) Paine conceived of a *sort of* social security
(1) Toussaint of a *kind of* nation-state
(4) Douglas suggested *maybe* a new constitution
(2) Hughes was *close enough* to the mass-popular approach to poetics as practiced by the Cuban Nicolás Guillén to be considered master conceptualist of—

(1-4) ESMERALDA

(4) When the jailer went to every cell marking with chalk the doors of the ones to be guillotined that morning, Paine's door was open, as a doctor had been visiting, and somehow in the confusion his door got marked on the inside, so that it later appeared to be closed

(3) The sound of a door ... swinging ... open ... where's that sound ... of a door ... swinging ... open ... coming from?

END OF PART 3

25

BALM TO BILK

A POETICS DIALOGUE FOR TWO VOICES

{voice 1, left margin; voice 2, center margin}

balm?

        balm . . . *and* buggin.

buggin already, uh?

        buggin.

and 'buggin's'
'balm' too?

        barely blurted,
        but true.

razzle!

        —is roust.

roust?

        'razzling' is 'rousting'.

wherefrom?

        balm.

'razzling' is 'rousting' from 'balm'?

        boldly blurted,
        but untrue.

——

bilk.

        huh?

'true' is 'bilk.'

        blick.

blick?

        I just blocked that—*blick.*

you can't . . . 'blick' that.

        blick.

'blick'
is 'blank.'

        baldly blurted,
        but not certain.

look, you live inside yourself like this
the outside *will watch you die!*

        ooh—bilk·bilk . . .

really.
but still, how rally
'balm' to 'roust' 'razzle'?
what *ought* the movement
brandish.

        '*brand*ish'?
        blithely blurted,
        but improbable.

but still, any formula
based purely on affect
outside of the realm of
objects, object's origins, relations

logics, counter-logics
nth degree determinations of—

      suckle-suckle.

'suckle' 'suckle'?

      mwah mwah mwah.

tsh . . . what? . . . *that*
modernist lily pond
boot-sloshing
containment?

      tsh . . . *that*
      ethical balm, morally brandishing
      splish-splash
      political razzle?

wuh-ho! *cry* of a tom cat!
a whale of a tail
on open seas . . .
rallying are we then, sister,
after all?

      'sister' in brotherhood!

'brother' in sisterhood!

      sloop to my sloop!

mainsail to my mid-mast!

      anchor to my—anchoring!

docking to my—dock!

      hey—yo, still roused to rule the gendered roost?

yo hey, still sloshing that
sassy death *inside*
brassily blurted?

some aquariums are just fabulous!
some aquariums are now cleaner and richer
than the authenticist flipped inside-out
luminescent
reef.

my point exactly.
through aesthetics, how *do* we
'bilk' to 'roust'
imperialist 'blicking'?

      that can be arranged, designed, well-represented . . .
      in an aquarium setting. *that* you're fancying to be
      flying fish, *outside* containment, feeding cycles
      boom & bust, is limbo-bimbo
      humble-mumble.

that's so . . . cryptic . . . so . . . *descendu* . . .

      sprung thighs though!
      I've got 'em
      I've got 'em—tactics—you know I do!

hmm . . . that's true.

    ——

    ——

should we talk agonistics?
new kinds of agonistic pleasures
to construct . . . pedagogic
massified praxii?

      sunken pirate ships it is . . .
      hide-outs, fantasy fortresses.

you're likening the movement's
structural potential
to an aquarium ornament?

collecting dusty nutrients . . .
plus, *effectively,* how to peekaboo
through ample portals, slithering motions
proportionate and changing scales of space
a sectoralized workforce—to de-sect
ready to both *blick* and *bilk*
ready to make *and* take *balms*—ours
terribly fully bodied.

oh . . .

      toy-lers, glimping, glumping, glad to be gloating.

huh?

      toy-lers, glimping, glumping, glad to be gloating.
      say it.

toy-lers

      —glimping.

glimping . . . glumping . . . glad to be gloating.

toy-lers glimping glumping galunking glad to be—*wait*
what *is* this?

      poetry. poetry for the movement.

poetry for the movement? this shit?

      what? not revolutionary enough for you?

nuh *uh,* can't blick me off like that, I mean,
where *are* the imbedded social demands
in this stuff?

      you mean, sly organelled movement
      partisanally nutritiated
      between roll-calling demands
      directed at gang-boss
      ain't body-body
      "massified praxii"?

uh . . . maybe we just don't speak the same language.

> uh, maybe that doesn't mean we're not part of
> the same movement.

true enough . . . what do you say we stroll to the seaside
catch an evening breeze, and pick it up there.

> sounds good. I could use the simulacral teasing
> cultural-specific shucking.

———
———

ah . . . that's nice, isn't it . . . this breeze . . . it's perfect
not warm, not cold, but cool against a warming sun.

> yeah . . . one thing about the sea is its
> flatness, its clarity of shape, its brisk
> unabashed filling of everything to its height
> (whatever that height may be, at any given time)
> then also there's the . . . how to put it . . . dumbness . . .
> a dumbness that's . . . intelligized . . . by us wanting it . . .

what.

> *the sea.*

oh . . . yeah . . . I agree.
something that's *not* mute
something that's *not* expressive
but something that's very much "us"
—in any language . . . and depending on the culture—

> 'balm' to 'bilk'?

ugh.

> just kidding.

no . . . maybe we *should* return to that . . .
a good time now, and great setting . . .
wavelets upon wavelets, constitutive
like these waters . . .

> what I meant was . . . that . . .
> to tend to 'balm,' that is,
> a social interpretive key,
> that if being *away from* body-body
> is 'roust'—coming *from* slavers
> (capitalist / imperialists) . . .
> is a 'rousting' *from*
> where we need to be . . .

tending to a *different kind of* . . . 'balm'?

> well, not overtly . . .
> that's a problem too, because
> 'overt' is 'razzle'
> always inviting of another 'razzle'
> . . . to 'roust' 'balm' that is . . .

oh . . . so you're saying 'balm' (ours) should be
as pure of a . . . *blick* . . . as can be?

> praise be flying fishes! you're getting it.

okay, but . . . can sometimes 'brandish' be the 'blick'
of the hour, in order to 'rally' the 'razzle'
needed to 'roust'?

> boldly blurted!
> but of course!

ah hah . . . *that's* why the special status of 'blurt'
can't have the enemy listening in at every turn.

> *exactement.* when they blurt, we brandish
> when they brandish, we blurt.

on the level of aesthetics you mean?

yes. but how do you pare the imperialist
from the imperialist aesthetic, and the imperialist aesthetic
from the imperialist? not an easy 'formula' as you say.

yeah okay . . . *whoa* . . . you're a trip!
who are you anyway?

      that's what I was wondering,
      who am we?

'who'
'am we' . . .
boldly blurted!

      but barely begun.

END OF DIALOGUE

PIG ANGELS OF THE AMERICLYPSE

AN ANTI-MASQUE FOR FOUR PLAYERS

Four players: can be of any age, gender, or accent.

Objects: one pencil, one hand-held yellow plastic sharpener/tumbler, something standing in for a "fax machine," blank sheets of "fax" paper.

Placements: table on far left stage with "fax machine" on top (P4's two "incoming faxes" are placed in front of blank stack of paper); P3 is stage right, P1 center, P2 stage left.

Initial Player Positions: P1, P2, & P3 sitting on knees looking straight forward; P4 walks up to each one and lays down their scripts directly in front of them (this is done in a careful, ceremonial manner); P4 also lays down tumbler and pencil in front of P3; P4 then steps to the side; after about 20 seconds, P1 plops down on hands and knees; P1 and P2 follow suit.

Initial Activity: for the next 30–40 seconds all three players alternate between a hands-and-knees position and laying flat on their stomach (legs active); the following activities for each player continue throughout entire play, unless otherwise instructed: P1 is inspecting the floor very carefully, focusing on minute things, pulling apart the ground (and script), spreading it, like picking through thick carpet looking for something; P1 alternates between this activity and putting his/her ear to the ground, straining to listen for something; P2 smushes small things on the ground (and script) with the tips of his/her fingers (later things are picked at with a pencil); P3 wipes the ground (and script) obsessively, like clearing a mirror, then looks at what's there, sees nothing, and returns to wiping and clearing; all players never turn to face one another, nor do they speak directly at one another, but rather remain locked into their activities. That is, their field of attention is directly below them.

Text in {brackets} is either contact zone/stage instructions or translation of text {not to be pronounced during performance}

—

{P1} The sun *the sun* . . . {P1 jolts back by glare; P2 & P3 straining to see it (directly below)}

{P2} And these puercos {snorts like a pig} {sneering} *sin destino.*

{P1} "Se busca"?

{P2} "Wanted"—"is sought"—"we seek"

{P1} Ah.

{P3 takes out a pencil; makes a gesture for each word (clearly visible to the spectators)}

Se busca—

lápiz	{"pencil"}
filoso	{"sharp"}
ambriento	{"starving"}

{P3 matter-of-factly, to no one in particular}

Se busca (por lo mínimo) un Brasileiro mas Mexicano que un Argentino Gringo.

{P2} And these puercos sin destino . . . *qué?*

{P1} The moon *the moon* . . . {P1 plunges head into the floor; P2 & P3 straining to hear it}

{P1, P2, & P3 continue their activities; P4 comes in from the side, heading toward the fax machine (on the table); P4 is not acknowledged by the others, as they can neither see nor hear P4; P4 is only slightly conscious of the others}

{P4} That can't be the whole of it, folks, come on.

{P3} Se busca—

        un fax   {pronounced 'fahks'}
        del Presidente

de la Republica!

{P4 begins fumbling with the machine; this continues throughout the play}

That's . . . if there's *ink* . . . in the Fax Toner

{P2} And these puercos . . . sin destino . . . *qué? qué?*

{P4} And . . . if I've re-ordered a back-up cartridge.

{P3 swoons, salivates, as if seeing an attractive body}

Un Canadiense—*cabrón!* {"kickass"}

Oof! Dual citizenship, *that's*

tight underwear.

{P1} —Too tight for me

{P2} —Oh my god

{P4 fiddling with machine} Is this thing even plugged in? Let's see.

{P1} The groom *the groom* . . .

{P2} We can't "marry" these— {snorts loudly several times} —*to one another!*

{P4} These presets . . . (tsk) I wonder if (tsk)

{P3 props up, sitting on knees, rolling pencil between palms of hands, in a slightly malicious tone; vowels in the words are extended, "milked"}

Se busca

lápiz	{"pencil"}
ambicioso	{"ambitious"}
vicioso	{"vice-prone"}

{P3 quits malicious manner and tone, then very matter-of-factly}

and a yellow tumbler

to screw it into.

{P3 takes out the tumbler, sharpens the pencil, then blows on it; P3 then touches the sharp tip}

{P1} The bride *the bride* {P2 & P3 straining to see it}

{P2} More slop more slop.

{P4} Tsk, I wonder if I even kept the receipt for it?

{P1} Oh my god—

{P2} Qué? Qué?

{P3} El Presidente de la Republica! {P1 & P2 straining to see it; again, P3 props up, sitting on knees, gesturing for each phrase, and drops back down after "to anyone"}

Se busca . . .
        hair gel (mucho)

y una tropa de poetas
worth a *culo*   {"ass"}
            "ambriento"
to anyone!

{P1 startled, pointing, with hands outspread, and increasingly agitated}

The sanctimonious hypocrite twilight

and its
           attendant northern
           sparkling cluster of
           —oh—wow

Shine *On!* Shine *On!*

{P4} I should have price-shopped it (tsk) I mean . . . oh well {P4 in the direction of the three, but not directly} (—hey, you folks down there getting a little antsy?)

{P2} Watch the gates! Watch those gates, now. The pretty pretty orange . . . *troughs.*

{P1} The bride *the bride*

{P2} We've already *established* "the bride"

{P1} Sorry

{P3 waving hand over ground, marveling}

Se busca

           —Cuddle Machines—

           —Octopi—

{P1 with ear to the ground} "I needn't budge an inch further" One of them just said that—d'ja hear it?

{P2 gestures erotically and grotesquely} I'm . . . *right here—right now* {springs up on two feet and lurches toward P3} give—me—that—lápiz . . . *ambriento.*

{P2 grabs pencil from P3, returns to position, and lowers it toward the floor, begins stabbing tiny moving things}

{P4} I *probably* should have checked into newer technology.

{P3} Which way's the sun again? Or the moon for that matter. I'm all *twisted* up.

{P1} Nationstate *up*—personal dreams *down*—got it?

{P2} These puercos, sin destinos . . . {as an aside} lively bunch.

{P3} {in singsong tone}

>"Ethos, lady sovereign, be not my decay!

>Tell me tell me

>Who are the *real* Americans of today?"

—What a beautiful songlet.

{P1 lowers ear to the floor} I can't hear it.

{P3 in singsong tone}

>"Ethos, lady sovereign, lend me some velour . . . "

>>—I've always liked velour
>>the touch, the feel of it—

{P2} {interrupts with a very loud snort}

{P1} The border *the border* . . .

{P2 & P3 straining to see it}

{P3} Se busca—

{P4} A fax—coming through!

{P3} "Paciencia"?

{P2} —"Patience"

{P3} —Ah.

{P4 reading a fax sheet from the machine; after reading the text out loud, continues silently (perplexedly) mouthing from it; P2 flat on the ground, with ear to the ground, does a complete circular rotation as the fax is being read}

From the . . . President . . . of the Republic (I'll be).

"Dear Sir / Madam,

With great uncomfortable and unfortunate condolence (my apologies dependent) is denial of transmitted acceptance, yours . . . for . . . Zero Card"

Zero Card?

{P2 looking at pencil, as if something's caught on the tip of it}

This is . . . {elongating the vowels} "desvaluado" {"devalued"}

{P1} What means {elongating the vowels} "desvaluado"?

{Structured Improvisation Activity: P2 springs up and walks towards P4; P4 and P2 speak to each other in a casual way, using their real names; the conversation is completely relaxed and revolves around recent travels they've both been on, stuff about crossing borders, all the paperwork involved, the lines, the barriers, etc, all completely improvised—for about 3 minutes; the conversation is digressive too, straying off into weird sub-topics, and eddies}

{P1 and P3 continue their respective activities, P1 ear to the ground straining to hear, P3 delighting at songlets she/he hears in the head, smiling, and often perplexed}

{Example of improvisation: "Hey-a Dan, my man, how was your trip to Canada?" "Cool cool, except, well, my Walmart card, you know, didn't uh, but the *Target* card, *plus* my visa to Serbia—"Serbo-Italians!? coming *out* of Kentucky, now, don't they have—" "yeah, a Starbucks card, in *this* instance, is uh, *helluh* . . . hellah better than a chain cutter on loan—*when you want it* (when you—" "you know what I want, Dan, like, right now" "Pyramidal Orientation" "a bucket of duty-free fried chicken" "for the road" "no, for here" "where's here?" "that's, that's the point, or for you, I'll say, *peak,* three sides to tumble down from" etc, etc.}

{Improvisation ends when one or the other gives the cue "geo-psychic traction" . . . i.e., "heard you got some much needed geo-psychic traction there" "psht, it appeared in my hand, just like that" "cool" "cool" "later" "yeah, later, man"}

{P2 plops back on the floor, picking at it with the pencil as before (unable to sense P4 in any way)}

{P1} The bride the bride the bride. The groom! (*I* can't tell which is which)

{P4 reading from another fax that just came through}

"Dear Sir / Madam,

Additionally, a downpour of pleasure mine, to bestow, for 28,000 Americos, upon receipt of here-be-said, Pick Five citizenship . . . in exchange for . . . Zero Card . . . wallet-size pic of me, bonus . . . {keeps silently and intently reading from the fax until next speaking part}

{P2} Slop, more slop for these . . . {in a high, sneering tone} *puercos de sus republicas.*

{P1 ear to the ground} "I needn't go a centimeter further"—d'ja hear that?

{P3 waving hand over ground, like a medium} Se busca . . . {matter-of-factly} un Nicaragüense with less of a Castroist mask than the most demasked Chilean, on any Sunday, liberal.

{P3 in a loud, hoarse, monotone voice; P1 and P2 looking at the floor, as if they're seeing something speaking}

"HI"

"HOW ARE YOU?"

"HOW'S YOUR FAMILY?"

"WHAT'S THE GRAPE SEASON LIKE THIS YEAR?"

"HOW *DO YOU* MANAGE

THE SLIGHT

CHANGE OF .

ACCENT?"

{All players throw themselves on their backs, arms and legs spread out, looking straight up}

{pause} {Players should take special care in emphasizing where the accent falls on each "Dario"}

{P1} Dário

{P2} Darío

{P3} Darió

{P2} Darió, okay.

{P3} No no, Darío it is.

{P2} I still think it's Dário.

{P1, P2, P3}

¡THANK YOU RUBÉN DARÍO!

{P1} For the options

{P3} Poetic palmistry

{P4} 28, 000 Americos!? Monster Pants! How can anyone manage that?

{P1 P2 and P3 pop up and link arm-in-arm with P4, as in a phalanx, facing the audience; they menacingly charge toward the spectators, stopping just short of collision}

{all four pulling and tugging on one anothers arms, weaving side to side}

{P2, defiant}

What
patch of earth

are these angels
overlooking?

{P3, defiant}

Defiant and sober

that's what

they look like.

{P1} Hell—is *me*, the way *I* feel.

{P4} Heaven you too {locks arms even tighter} (here, now) and *me*,
purged of all *practical* purgatory—cripes . . . what kind of art-form
is this?

{all 4 players}

¡THAT CAN'T BE THE WHOLE OF IT, FOLKS, COME ON!

{P1, P2, and P3 plop back on the floor, facing up; P4 returns to the
fax machine and snatches fax after fax (each one blank) throwing
them to the floor after a brief inspection of each sheet (continues
doing this until next speaking part)}

{P1} Nationstates *up*—personal dreams *down.*

{P2} and mugs

{P3} mugs

{P1} mugs

{P2} mugs

{P3} mugs

{pause}

{P1, P2, P3, slowly, in a semi-sleep state}

{P1} All I see is . . . The Great Divide.

{P3} I am the heat.

{P2} The wanderlust . . . where'd it go?

{P1} "Solo se que dios es Bolivariano"—I just heard that.

{P2} Puerqueros Hammer.

{P4 frustrated, loses interest in machine, knocks it off the table}
Psh!

{P4 slowly walks to where the other three are and joins them in prostate position}

{Pause}

{All four players (very slowly, calmly, peaceably) act as themselves, addressing each other using their real-life names}

{P2} That's good, [Jocelyn], . . . it's good you're happy . . .

{P3} So happy . . . the nest of some missing pretty baby I am . . .

{P1} Delighted is a goofy word {chuckles softly} . . . jazzed . . . is only a little less goofy {all four chuckle softly}

{P3} You're here, [David], right . . . some . . . far-off . . . *other* time {all four chuckle softly}

{P4} Borders . . . silent wars . . . mirth . . . gloom.

{P2} Vogue, what's in vogue.

{P3} May . . . *be* . . . that, [Stephanie], . . . *that*

{P1} The way out?

{P2} Art goes art goes

{P3} Away . . .

{P2} And back . . .

{P1} In . . .

{P3} And out . . .

{P4}   "Yo persigo una forma que no encuentra mi estilo,
botón de pensamiento que busca ser la rosa" •

I pursue a form that doesn't find my style,
mind's stem that strives to be the rose

{P2} Contrive
                 identify
the themelets
                 variate

{P3} Se busca . . .

{P1} Songlets of sorts, yeah?

{P4} Yeah . . .

{P2} Mm hmm . . .

END OF ANTI-MASQUE

• lines from Rubén Darío's "Yo persigo una forma" ("I seek a form")

(English translation, R. Toscano)

HUMANA ANTE OCULOS

AN ANTI-MASQUE FOR THREE PLAYERS

Players: *P1, P2, M (master of ceremonies), volunteer from the audience; all three players (plus volunteer) can be of any age, gender or accent*

Objects: *a cape, two large placards (one reads,* DEUS NOVUM, *the other,* Runaway Ideas Rule the World*), two cups of confetti (preferably shiny) placed side by side in the performance space, about three feet apart; two large strips of velcro*

{P1, wearing a cape, twirling, gliding, prancing (and always re-composing body at every strophe); P2 looking on nonchalantly from afar}

{P1}

Mars of
          mournful
final
          rocky
resting
          places

Venus of
          vapor hot
sultry
        fleeting
surfaces

Pluto proves
          a distant object's
tug
however slight
          towards the center

My peeps
buck
in saturnalia

           I beg Mercury
for a speedier response-time
mimesis?

Failed Exit Strategy

       Representation
is escalation

{P1 whips off the cape and flings it to the ground}

{P2 stands directly next to P1 (but not looking at P1, and in an
aggressive rapid tone)}

You can disassemble an RPG-7V in the thick of night, break it
into four parts, stuff it into a sack, less than 20 lbs, glide by
checkpoint, angry sprite.

Without the spray of glorious daylight, *other* sprite—can't find
his prick, confuses aim-tip with firing pin, likely to back-bust,
retro-madre . . . *en la madre* . . . {P2 turns to P1, and extends hand}
lieutenant, your hand.

{P1 puts out a hand, tentatively, and then withdraws it in horror;
P1's hand ends up in a palm-out position (facing the spectators),
so as to "transfer" the "energy" to M}

{M with hand raised, approaches one spectator for each word; M
places his/her hand on the specator's hand before saying each
word; this is done in a calm, stately manner; M should remain
unpredictable as to who M might touch}

       FEMININE

MASCULINE

EMASCULINE

FEMASCULINE

MASCUFEMASCULINE

FEMIFEMASCULINE

EFEMIFEMASCULINE

MASCUMASCUFEM

FEMFEMIMASCFEM

MASCUEFIMIMASC

{P2}

Ask no questions

The Special Op is at 11:00 am sharp

ACE of
CRUSADER
fuss

{P1 quickly picks up the cape and flings it high and away}

{P2}

hallowed white light of
gray clay
stuffed
hiss

currency of

zero

ONE
  is captured—

           The voltage
—is undependable

but the lust—*nay*

           New Information
           New
In
Formation

{M walks into the space (from one side to the other; then stopping
at center) holding a large placard towards the audience that reads}

DEUS NOVUM

{P1 and P2 get behind M (to the left and right respectively)
disputing with each other (silently), pointing to things behind the
placard, as if decoding an ancient alphabet}

{P1 and P2 stop disputation, reach for two cups and begin
gracefully spreading confetti on the floor, each saying "fulmina"
(one can speak over the other, overlapping; activity is not to be
rushed).

fulmina
        fulmina

fulmina
        fulmina

fulmina
        fulmina

fulmina
        fulmina

{P2, with head raised high, straining to see what's behind the audience, gestures with hand}

The bright stained glass, warm
color washes the quiet listener's face

lulls-it-at-the-point-of-waking-it, *faith*

(soft faith, faint faith)

{with suddenness, and pointing to one side}

—smashes through the western atrium!

{gestures toward confetti on the ground}

commanders of a half-million fragments

e n t r a n c e

{steps right up to P1, but doesn't look at P1}

Art Pimp
with a full clip:

{P1 thundering, as if to someone present}

"move, you!"   "sit!"

"stand!"   "spread 'em!"

{M carries a placard from one end of the space to the other; the placard reads}

Runaway Ideas Rule The World

{P1 gets on knees; P2, with outstretched arm, pointing at P1}

{P2}

Niño
          all grown up

Niño
        tremulous

bears down {P2 pushes P1's shoulders down, then walks a bit in
the direction of the spectators}

not like in the movies
not like at State Department private party moods

{P2 points to P1, again, this time accusingly}

{P2}

nasce te ipsum   "know thyself"

Bowery Poetry Club, NYC, Spring 2006

{P1 stands up and animatingly enacts what P2 is saying}

. . . glides toward the bar counter . . .

. . . achieves eye contact . . .

. . . nods for the usual . . .

{"Tomb of Sargon" songlets are read by M; songlets are well-
articulated according to line breaks}

> *Tomb of Sargon*
> *is deep, undiscovered*
> *and unstirred*

. . . analyzes the situation . . .

discriminates between

slipstreams and eddies of—

> *Tomb of Sargon*
> *might contain*
> *a few jewels, hard*
> *as Sargon*

... interventionist artwork ...

a decision is made
to fully engage—

> *Tomb of Sargon*
> *fascinating*
> *for students of*

{P1 suddenly blurts out, as if possessed}

Elementary sex!
Elementary bliss!
Elementary torment!

Beads of sweat
                     on your artifacts
are appreciated!

(mild spasms of the belly
                           also)
{P2 continues}

... is almost instantly

cornered ...

{P1 squats and covers ears as if an explosion is about to occur}

{after 20 seconds of P1 squatting, P2 says}

New Information

{P1 pops up and starts (along with P2 and M) applauding enthusiastically
in the direction of the spectators (inducing them to join in); all say}

omne gens plaudit

> *omne gens plaudit*

omne gens plaudit

omne gens plaudit

omne gens plaudit

{applause slows, then stops}

{M very slowly rips apart the giant strips of Velcro}

{P2}

Rotator kneecap twisting in true-velcro sound

{P1 suddenly holds knee in agony}

{P1 then hurriedly retrieves cape and puts it on, sets up (taking time), and twirls, quixotically as before; P2 looking on nonchalantly)

{P1}

Jupiter of
         citizen·big
orbitry of
         micro
clandestine
        basura

Neptune of
         emerald·distant
lonely
    costly
enlightenment

Uranus
     of
stand·alone
     stray·elliptical
              direction
—*talk to me baby*

{P1 flings off the cape, falls to the ground, holding knee, grimacing}

{at this point a volunteer spectator, someone who has been taking pictures, jumps in and begins hurriedly snapping P1 holding knee; volunteer does activity as if in great bodily danger (about to get shot, blown up, etc.)}

{P2, while volunteer is "snapping pics"}

Lieutenant, your hand

{P1 confused, unable to hear P2}

{P2}

Lieutenant, your hand

{volunteer now runs away from P1; P1 pops up and starts acting in a hip gallery schmoozy way—hugs, double-cheeked kisses, etc.}

{P2, unaffected looks at P1 doing antics to the air, then walks off}

{P2}

Lulls you at the point of waking you, *faith*

(soft faith, faint faith)

{M holds up the **DEUS NOVUM** placard; M continually tries to cover up P1's antics with the placard (print facing the audience); P1 persists in glad-handing mode striving to peek out from behind the placard, trying to get a glimpse of the audience; peek-a-boo activity lasts for a good while; M finally and swiftly withdraws placard, from which they both exit the Contact Zone}

END OF ANTI-MASQUE

ECO-STRATO-STATIC

A RADIO POETICS PLAY IN ONE ACT FOR THREE VOICES

VOICES: regular font, *italics*, **bold**

—

elements:

**a wall of flames,
a big blue ball
on one side of it;**

**an entity,
another entity,
several more entities.**

{pause}

Hurl it over.

I can't—it's too heavy.

Get help.

I can't—everyone's too busy.

Scream to see if anybody responds.

Scream what?

HELP.

Okay.

Is anyone responding?

Not a one, responding.

Start acting like you have an innovative product.

Okay.

What's happening?

I'm acting like I have an innovative product.

Is anybody coming?

No.

Put on a happy-pappy face.

Got it.

Is anybody coming?

I see somebody.

Somebody coming?

Somebody coming.

Say something.

What?

HELP.

Okay.

What's happening now?

They're talking to me about an innovative product.

What is it?

Some kind of art-thing.

Can it be fashioned into a lever, or a ramp?

I'll ask'em.

What do they say?

"Depends on how you look at it."

Tell them you're out of time.

Okay.

What do they say?

They want to know if I have financial backing.

Escort them to the wall.

Escorting—in progress.

What's going on now?

They've walked into the wall of flames.

What did they say?

Aaaah!

Start dancing.

Okay—dancing. I'm dancing . . . still dancing . . . still.

Do you see anybody dancing?

No.

Put on a happy-pappy face.

Got it.

Do you see anyone dancing?

Yes—yes I do.

Keep dancing.

I'm dancing—with a happy-pappy face.

What's going on now?

They're dancing my way.

Keep dancing.

Dancing—big time.

Now put on a desperate face.

Got it.

What's happening?

They're dancing away.

Back to the happy-pappy.

Got it.

What now?

They're coming back.

Ask them if they can help.

Okay.

Can they help?

No.

Why not?

They say it's not their specialty, cup of tea.

Ask them what is.

Okay.

What do they say?

Innovative ideas, images, looks, designs.

Tell them that if they help to get the big blue ball over the flaming wall, there'll be a prize in it for them.

Alright.

What do they say?

They want to know what the prize is.

Tell them LIFE.

Okay.

What do they say?

They say they want it up front.

Gyrate toward the wall.

Gyration—in progress.

What's happening?

They're following.

You know what to do.

Done.

What's going on now?

The billowing flames of the wall are cascading down the underbelly of the big blue ball. Wait.

What is it?

One of them left the art-thing behind.

What kind of thing is it—exactly?

Hundreds of printed sheets of paper, bound together into an almost perfect cube.

What does it say?

"A Gentle Knight was pricking on the plaine,
Y cladd in mightie armes and silver shielde,
Wherein old dints of deepe wounds did remaine,
The cruell markes of many' a bloudy fielde—"

Stop. . . . What else?

"Yet armes till that time did he never wield:
His angry steede did chide his foming bitt,
As much disdayning to the curbe to yield:
Full jolly knight he seemd, and faire did sitt,
As one for knightly giusts and fierce encounters fitt."

Scream for help.

Okay.

Anyone coming?

No.

Can the thing be fashioned into a lever, or a ramp?

"But on his brest a bloudie Crosse he bore,
The deare remembrance of his dying Lord,
For whose sweete sake that glorious badge he wore,
And dead as living ever him ador'd:"
 —Hardly.

Hurl it into the wall.

Done.

Look up.

I'm looking up.

Do you see any rain?

No.

Unfurl your umbrella.

Done.

Is it raining now?

Yes.

Proclaim the end of cause and effect.

Done.

What's happening?

Millions of them are coming my way.

What do they look like?

Reverential.

Ask them if they can help.

Okay.

What do they say?

Not a one—can help.

Why not?

They want to see the umbrella & rain thing again.

Tell them no.

Done.

What now?

They're dispersing—in silence.

Unfurl your umbrella.

Unfurled.

Is it raining?

No, but they're coming back.

Furl in your umbrella.

Furled in.

Are they still coming?

They're getting closer.

Read from the thing.

"Upon a great adventure he was bond,
That greatest Gloriana to him gave,
That greatest Glorious Queene of Faerie lond,
To winne him worship, and her grace to have,
Which of all earthly things he most did crave—"

Pause . . . go on.

"And ever as he rode, his hart did earn
To prove his puissance in battell brave
Upon his foe, and his new force to learne;
Upon his foe . . . a Dragon horrible and stearne."

What's happening? What's happening now?

They're forming into groups.

What kind of groups?

One is calling itself The Administrators (Group A), the other (Group B) can't quite decide on a name. Group A is busy cataloging, scheduling, surveillancing. The other is . . . well! Well, well not exactly really but—

Proclaim—The Beginning—of Self.

All right.

Is anyone saying anything?

Not a word.

Proclaim—The End—of Self.

Okay.

Anyone saying anything now?

I see a few specs in Group B starting to twinkle.

Dance.

How?

In the approximate rhythm of their twinkling.

Okay.

Anything happening?

The twinklers are forming into their own group—Group C.

Do they have a spokesperson?

I can't tell.

Dangle a giant mic from a giant crane.

Done.

Is anybody approaching?

One of them is hanging from the mic, swinging on it, back and forth.

That's your spokesperson.

I figured that much.

Say something.

What?

Ask for help.

No.

. . . .

. . . .

I said no. No . . . hey . . . I said, I said no. Do you hear me? I said—

Yo! Do I have to swing on this thing all day to get your attention?

Uh . . . Oh! . . . hang on.

Hang on!? Whadya think I'm a trapeze artist here? Whadya think this is a circus? Who're you—Bozo, the Existentialist?

Uh . . .

My people are getting antsy over here. You wanna show—you don't wanna show. You call for a show—you don't wanna show—

I . . . I want a show . . . I want . . . a show.

Alrighty then! What do you want—you want bungee sticks, guillotines, AK-47's, car bombs, hemlock pot roast, moonseed muffins—what do you want—spit it out.

A lever and/or ramp would be nice ... pre•fer•ably.

Prefubly.

Yes, pre•fer•ably.

Prefubly.

That's what I said.

You got an extra syllable there.

Uh—do you have some sort of license, or degree, or some kind of certificate, for this kind of work?

Listen, Bozo, you proclaim the End of Self as a *Beginning* of Self, across an axis of Presence / Absence, as an ideo-somatic registry for an onto-episto paratactic—to get your prophylactic—to work— *for peanuts!* WE'RE OUTTA HERE!!

Wait, no. Don't. Oh ... oh no ... (damn!)

A Gentle Knight was pricking on the plaine,
Y cladd in mightie armes and—

Hey! Where the hell have you been? Were you here the whole time? Did you hear all that?

The whole bloody thing.

Why didn't you step in—lend counsel, direction, why didn't you, after all, HELP?

I wanted to clear your mind—of one word, once and for all.

What word?

One, that when not casting its terminal tunnel vision, that the high wall of flames might lower down to the height of say, shag carpet.

What word?

So that the big blue ball might with the slightest effort, through simple love, be rolled over—to the other side (being the near perfect sphere that it is).

That it is, that it is. But, what word?

Be still, I'll whisper it to you.

Nice. Trust me, it's cleared. Clean.

Good.

But now you've got me snagged up on "simple love."

Simple love, yes, a simple (reverential) love—of life itself; basic technology, like flint-tips, pottery, the wheel, the lever and/or ramp; a millennia to develop it, a millennia to destroy it at the same time.

Not like "econ—"

No. Development, in the true sense, borne of the body, resilient, hard to market.

And not like "help."

No. "Help," in our epoch, too readily invites knights, crosses, swords . . . dragons . . . Faerie Lond.

Faerie Lond. I'll try to come to grips with that.

You do that.

I will.

Good.

Good.

Good.

Good.

END OF RADIO PLAY

FIRST BOX

A POETICS THEATER PLAY

Setting: "a campfire at evening"

Objects: logs in a pile, two low stools, two poking sticks, a styrofoam cup, a pink wig, a small stuffed-animal squirrel, a long string tied around it.

Players can be of any age, gender, or accent; A in regular font; B in *italics;* C ("string-puller") as marked.

Space directions are in [brackets]; underlined words are emphasized throughout.

•

> [A & B both sitting around a campfire, facing each other, poking it with sticks]

I'm thinking about how the first
>>> ape-of-us
>> first
>> put together
> a box.

It must have (at first) been
>> a half, or two-thirds box, or

maybe (by accumulated chance,
or accelerated accident), a hollow log
>>> at the edge of the camp
screamed out—"box!"

I mean a box, man.

Four sides, 90 degree angles—the works.

> [B stands up, paces around the fire; at every 45-degree angle, speaks these four lines]

"It must have bink—"
"It could have klappened—"
"It is klikely—"
"It is quinceivable—"

This
            at the edge of the camp
            rhe-TOR-ic
This
            neatly placed
            artsy filth

is what we <u>know</u>
            about the "first" box?

                    [sits]

I thought
It
Had passed
Into a
Box
That

What?

This
essence-precedes-the-thing
Play-TONIC Thought.

Though it's a fact, some still say

            [B stands, and slowly, constructively, composes
            body into arm-outstretched position]

            "uphold!"

Marx-Lenin-Mao-Tse-Tung

            [breaks the position, and before sitting on stool, says]

            <u>Thought.</u>

Though it's also a fact, the entire province of Guangdong
(with a population a third of the entire U.S.)

is in open revolt
against

> [gets on all fours, head down, with raised fist, in a
> weeping tone]

"To get rich is glorious!"

> [sits down next to A, and very soberly]

—Thought.

You talking about <u>la fracture sociale</u>, ape?

I thought
It
Had passed
Into a
Box
That

What?

This
thing-precedes-the-essence
                              ape-of-us
not entirely satisfying the

> [lightly pokes B with stick]

<u>physical</u> requirements of
                              global capital
—disciplining.

There might well <u>be </u>
a five-sided box
that can be "upheld"

> [A stands, walks directly up to the spectators]

The image is one of several ape-of-us <u>mentally</u> holding up
a five-sided box, and grunting

[throughout the piece, A & B abruptly and simultaneously say the
phrase "my space!" with arms flung out wide in a "Guernica" ·like
horrified face gesture; both instantly recover from the extreme gesture]

"<u>my</u> space!"

[pause] [B staring off into space, but with
conviction]

The daylight grows dim.

The feast around the fire
is set to go.

The nouns are verbing.

The "accidents"
are about to begin.

That much is true!

What
Much
Is
True?

That
"as the light grows dim"

"a five·sided box"

is
about to
<u>enspace</u>

its contents

I thought
that's what you—

                    [vocal burst is very rapid; A and B alternate, but
                    can also overlap; sequence can be lengthened]

thought *said* said *thought* thought *said* thought

I'm saying,
the third, half, two-thirds, <u>and</u>
regular old
four-sided—

                    [vocal burst as before]

box *play* play *box* box *play* box

can be—
                    [burst]

fawned over buried deep *fawned over* buried deep *fawned over* buried
deep

                    [pause] [B, facing spectators]

By accumulated chance (or accelerated accident),
                    we see the ancient-future ritual
Unfolding before our very eyes.

What we thought was progressive camp was repressive culture,
                    what we thought was regressive culture was
                    progressive camp,
Logs are logs, however.

It is quinceivable that each of us might know a no-spacer
                    too quinced to confête in the info-fire;
It is a brute fact, to be perfumed?

Much poetry is aerating at the foothills of Helicon;

                    [C quickly slides the squirrel by the string
                    across the space]

a lively little orange squirrel captures our attention (aah);
Voyez! a lot of BOX—is simply burning up!

[rapidly]

—scream
        —*confusion*
—result?
        —*think*

[A & B both walk to the back of the area, backs
facing the spectators; both looking up]

I'm thinking about how the first
                        ape-of-us
                learned how to dance
in concert (instead of—<u>verklempt</u>)

at the foothills of a forbidden mountain.

It must have (at first) been
                        quite the freakout, or randy encounter, and

maybe (by accumulated chance,
or accelerated accident), a wizened warlock
                        berdache of the camp
shouted—"jump!"

[A facing B]

I mean a boogie-down, man.

<u>All</u> the genders, <u>all</u> the tricks

—mc'twists to mc'tumbles.

[pause] [both walk back and sit around the campfire in the
same positions as at the beginning]

[slowly]

I thought

78

the fire

had leapt

into the

pan

or was it

the pan

that had

fired up

the

                    [rapidly]

—fawn
            —*convulsion*
—revolt?
            —*kink*

  A third the size eh . . . Texafornica?

                [A still sitting, to the spectators]

the nouns
are <u>nouning</u>

gloriously!

Fact is, apey,
            the open revolt
is too brutish
            for your—voyez!
"enspacement"

The cybertronic stats
        —are in!

Staples
        on the open flesh
of closed revolt

Skimp
        on "humaneness"
and that's
        art?

rhe-TOR-ic reproduction
        and that's—

—planned-arbitrary
        thunkery . . .

200 million unemployed . . . with no pensions.

It is a brute fact, not to be . . . eau de . . . <u>toileted</u>.

                [squirrel is tossed out into the space, and reeled back;
                A & B, deadpan]

Squirrel aside
        —squirrel aside

This
thing-precedes-the-thing
                —preceding some other thing

it's
as if
                [simultaneously]

"*my* space!"
had—

                [B jumps off stool, in full "rocker" mode]

80

—strum strum,
drum a drum drum—strum
drum

—fuzzblurr!
      powerchord

dzzzzh—turururu!

dzzzzh—turururu!

LOVE HARD!!!

      [B plops to the floor; A, calmly]

. . . what else . . .

      [A gets up, unhurried, and sits back on stool]

I'm thinking about how the first
                         ape-of-us
            first
            took apart
      a box.

It must have (at first) been
                  a two-hundred percent
        overkill
        kind of

        affair

till someone
in the camp (high)

        hollered

"no box—no meal"

(it's
as if
        [simultaneously]

"<u>my</u> space!"
had—)

Aah . . . this
thing-precedes-the-thing
excrescence of an
                              "accident"

Ain't it a—
                    (no-key
                    cause the no-lock
                    cause the no-hatch—no-how
                    fifth side
                    sought)
<u>*bitch?*</u>

                    [pause]

—collapsed, as if,

                    [simultaneously]
"<u>my</u> space!"

had collapsed . . .
while expanding at the same time

                    [squirrel is thrown onto the space where A is sitting]

                    (<u>what</u> the—

It eats the refuse left by hipsters

and retreats
into a hollow log

at eventide.

Creative writing programs aside

                    [A kicks it]
                                        —aside

...what else...

80 million gray-haireds will rely on 40 million pink-haired

unemployds

A prize
in every specially marked box.

Planned-arbitrary
multi-subjectivity.

[pause] [A pokes styrofoam cup with stick and raises it]

At the foothills of the Poconos ... is a Dunkin Donuts
I can't seem to scrub from my mind

[B undoes pants and lowers ass over the fire]

(<u>what</u> the—

dzzzzh—tururururu!

dzzzzh—tururururu!

[B calmly puts pants back on and sits] [pause]

I'm thinking about how the first

ape-of-us
first
put together

a comprehensive

donut marketing strategy plan for all of Pennsylvania

[A flinches back, expecting B to repeat the ass-to-fire antic;
B slowly cranes neck forward; and slowly, markedly]

d z z z h—tu ru ru ru

"It must have bink—"

d z z z h—tu ru ru ru

"planned·arbitrary thunkery"

                    [B stands up and walks toward the "mountainside," back
                    to the spectators, looking up]

Aren't you just an aging adjunct?

Poetaster, add.

Enspacer of pain, add.

                    [walks back to A with a newfound (contained) bubbliness]

In the style of a Grungerian chant
we should chant...now...together...in concert...

Aren't <u>you</u> just an aging
                        McHomo
                              Cogitans
pan·fried
            monkey?

[with hands clasped like a monk, in a low voice, grunting]

Glooooo-riiii-aaaaaa

1974.

What?

I thought
It
Had passed
Into a
Box
That

What?

This
ever-shrinking
                ancient-future
ritual of
      "indie"
      sexpression

mc'fumbles
and mc'quips

      of

economic
      confidence

          [B walks directly up to the audience]

The image is one of several ape-of-yous
                     flying over the pyre
clasping your
      curled up tootsies

      [walking away from spectators]

(it's not my fault)

      [with raised fist, half sarcastically]

(love hard)

      [rapidly]

—screech
      —illusion
—convert?
      —pink

      [pause] [B, returning to the campfire, standing;
      A, looking up at the stars]

Purple-lipped Saturday nights

—of the seventies

and Malloy

                    [nostalgically]

(One Adam 12 Malloy, Sammy's Malloy,
Malloy's Fish n' Tackle, Malloy's Wigs n' Things)

—bingin' in your head

          no internet
          no flames
          no cybertronic stats

Tooh-TOR-ic

                    [with clenched fist, making a muscle]

"we mean it man!"

What
do we know

about the "first" punk?

Blanched by the books
they weren't.

                    [B, very matter-of-factly]

It might have been their fault . . . it is quinceavable.

                    [A, grimacing]

1989.

What?

I thought
the leaping
had puffed out
the pyre

Or was it
the pyre
had puffed <u>up</u>
the leaping?

[to the spectators]

*The verbs
are <u>verbing</u>*

gloriously!

Voyez!

The first ape-of-us
probably <u>needed</u>
a box—

[B, clasping hands again]

Glooooo-riiii—

to enspace
its contents

dzzzzh—tururururu!

It's the contents
that loves hard.

Tururururu!

[B calmly fits A with a pink wig]

The ape-of-us . . . how <u>far</u> we've come.

What
do we know

about the first

camping equipment sales-ape?

—

END OF POETICS THEATER PLAY

CORDONED

A BODY MOVEMENT POEM FOR FIVE PLAYERS AND ONE READER

The text can be read out loud at the performance, or played from a recording. The tempo of the text is very slow (ellipses are observed, line breaks and spaces are observed). The volume of the words varies from very soft (parenthesis) to loud (all caps). Words in <brackets> are pronounced an octave higher than normal voice (something between a falsetto and a hiccup). The intonation of the poetic lines surges sometimes with an inward psychic motion (reaching for deeper, more hidden layers of realization), and sometimes with an outward motion (as if expelling the most immediate demons). The overall disposition of the reader is as one who is always utterly alone.

The text is usually read before an action. The exceptions and corresponding indicators are the following: "•" denotes action (done and completed) before text, "≈" denotes simultaneous occurrence of text and action.

Players hold indicated positions until prompted to take others. Original "positions" (for four main players) are marked by an 'x' on the Contact Zone/Area/stage floor; a line (left to right) is also marked ¾ of the way down the space; four equidistant spots on the line are marked; center space is also marked.

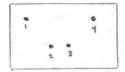 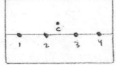

First position marked   Line marked with places (and "center")

"Neutral stance" denotes player standing straight with hands on the front of thighs, relaxed and ready to spring into action (though not in an "at ready" stance, as in service to someone).

Lines on score indicate conceptual episode, not breaks in timing (or spacing) of performance.

Video clips that have been prepared are cued up at the beginning of the performance. The clips are as follows: "masses gathering" (app. 10 seconds), "empty chairs" (app. 8 seconds), "blue sky with clouds" (app. 4 seconds), "masses on the move" (app. 8 seconds), "imperialist forces on the move" (app. 14 seconds), flash of same image (app. 2 seconds), "empty chairs (in reverse order)" (app. 8 seconds).

•

There . . . I've roped off **(1-4 in their primary position, in neutral stance)**

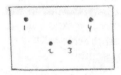

all mistakes, follies, dumb shows of . . .

"feeling"

Motored Movement

surrender   **(3 walks forward)**

why always . . . **(3 stops)**
some . . .   **(3 takes stance; left knee on the ground, right arm raised high with a clenched fist (not theatrical, but matter-of-fact)**

one . . .

powered mistakes! *powered* follies! *powered* shows of . . .

feeling . . .

all over . . . **(3 bends torso over, "collapsed," arms dangling)**
showering . . .
all over . . .

all <it!> **(3 flings right arm up; (relaxed) wrist leads the action)**

over <it!> **(3 flings left arm up)**

feeling <it!> **(3 flings head upwards)**

(. . . all over it . . .) **(3 torsos re-collapse; arms dangling)**

¡OH DON'T MIND ME! **(• 4 does two-arm (broad-reaching)
windmill motion; stops at "me!")**

I've been living, *at best*

kind present . . .

the passage is cruel . . . **(3 stands up, hand-on-hip casual)**

so I've roped it off . . . there . . .

minimal show . . .

(so *old* skool
to say 'old skool')

surrender **(3 walks back to original position)**

93

why always . . .

one . . .   **(1 & 2 each walk to the other's spot)**

as by two . . . **(1 & 2 walk back to original positions)**

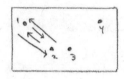

why never (*and* forever)

one

as by . . .

---

oh, the combos . . .   **(1–4 each walk to the middle line**
(each in their line spots) and face
forwards, in neutral stance)

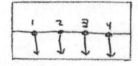

the combos they're . . . what are they?

not-here not-*not*-here   **(1–4 put hands out in front as if to**
grab something (once))

not-here not-*not*-here . . . **(1–4 pull hands in back into**
neutral stance (swiftly, but
not dramatically)

there . . .   **(2 & 4 turn & face each other (no walking))**

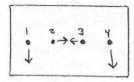

I could stare . . .

at that stare . . .

perfect . . .

so . . .

I know what I know cause I *feel*
I don't feel . . .

"perfect"   **(1 & 4 face backwards, 2 & 3 face to the
                 sides, away from each other)**

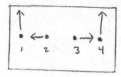

I've been living, *at best*

passable present
of passable past . . .

hole . . .

deepening . . .

tomorrow . . .

rope it off . . .   **(beginning with 1, then 2, and so forth, each swiftly sweeps their arm in a downward arcing motion (same arm for all, right or left, all in the same direction) as if releasing a rope onto the ground; when each is in maximally (arm & spine) stretched-out stance, they hold the form)**

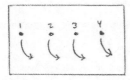

to be masterful . . . rope it off . . .

all misfangled follies, smart shows of . . .

I <it!> defy <it!>

I <it!> <it!> <it!>

who . . .   **(2 breaks form and hops three times forward and towards the center)**

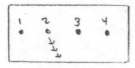

in the hole

decides . . .

"start the reading now"   **(1, 3, 4 vacate the stage; 1 to right side, 3 & 4 to the left side; 2 goes into neutral stance)**

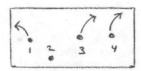

—*whatever!*

(whatever, man, whatever)

masterful . . . mystery . . .   **(• 2 with arms crossed, in casual**
                                        stance, fingers tapping)

I've roped it off . . . right . . . along . . . here . . . a little bend . . . a semi-
loop . . . a . . .

spec?   **(CLIP (10 sec.) of protesting masses gathering**
          into an area [note: author's (2007) political intent
          is to show a pro *proceso* / Chavez rally in
          Venezuela])

power spec! (context . . .)   **(clip off)**

coil it in coil it in   **(≈ 2 one arm out to grab, then pulls it in)**

Motored Movement   **(2 walks off stage and sits with the**
                          spectators)

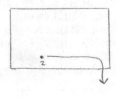

. . .
. . .

see?   **(Entire Area Vacated)**

I feel what I feel cause *I know*
I can't know

"here" . . .   **(CLIP (8 sec.) of empty auditorium chairs,
followed by empty stadium chairs, then empty
chairs around a dining table, an empty bed; clip off)**

betimes . . . so old skool . . . "feeling" . . . showering . . . minding . . .

that stare . . .   **(CLIP (4 sec.) of bright blue sky with white clouds
(at zenith))**

coil it . . . **(clip off)**

(out! . . . out)

I've been . . .

_____

¿PERFECT START TO THE READING, HUH?   **(≈ 1-4 walk back onto the
stage and begin pacing ran-
domly over it (not chaotic
and not too fast); each player
has come up with a (secret)
reason of their own as to
why such random roaming)**

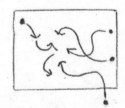

now what . . . **(1–4 freeze)**

power hole . . . mystery . . . deepening . . . right . . . along . . . this . . . "s" . . .
curve . . . a . . . an . . . an . . . an uneven . . . tangent . . . or . . . ray . . . a ray
. . . of . . . from . . . one . . . some one . . . vortice . . . center . . .

(≈ 1–4 begin roaming over the area again)

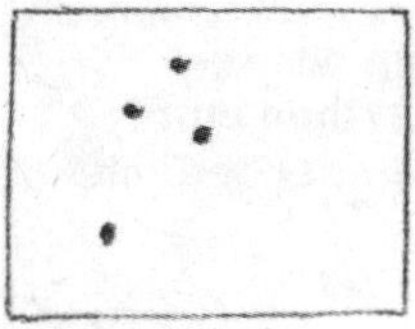

“to be masterful . . . ”

(≈ 1–4 freeze)

<it!>

suck it up

Motored Movement

who . . .

who decides?

who decides . . .

---

the combos . . .

(1–4 smush together / “puppy-pile” on the ground in a circle)

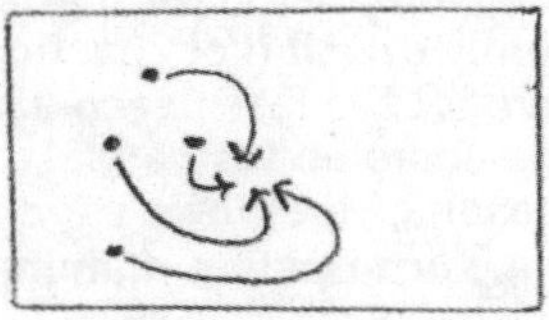

what are they?

always . . .

one as . . . by another . . .

why never . . . one . . . as by . . .

by gosh . . .　　**(CLIP (18 sec.) of masses on the move, in the**
　　　　　　　　same direction (as in a wide boulevard))

spec . . . another . . .

. . .
. . .

all these all these (context . . .) **(clip off)**

(3 starts rolling away toward down-left stage (diagonally))

triple-slip
　　　sloop
　　　　　slider
　　　　　　knot . . . *tie'em up tie'em up*　　**(3 freezes)**

for dead Caesar's crumbling marbled shithouse—　**(≈ 1, 2, 4 pop**
　　　　　　　　　　　　　　　　　　　　　up with arms
　　　　　　　　　　　　　　　　　　　　　akimbo, facing
　　　　　　　　　　　　　　　　　　　　　forward)

rope it up . . . at the base . . .

"feeling" . . . dumb show . . . .

unsurrendering . . . edifice . . .

(. . . jarring silence . . .)

I hear what I hear cause *I think*
what I can't ... "think"

**(3 props up arms raised high
over head, almost levitating, on
tiptoe, stretched out maximally,
though not tense)**

perfect ...

**(1, 2, 4 all lower to the ground to
listen to it, each with one ear)**

hole ...

siphoning ...

send thy vapors up <it!>

(... bathe, baby, bathe, bathe ...   **(≈ 3 into neutral position)**

bob on up ... pickled thoughts ...)

I grab what I grab cause I grip— **(1, 2, 4 grip the air in front of them)**

(grip ...)   **(1, 2, 4 stop gripping)**

---

ah ... the combos ... I release ... here ... a tug ... a little wiggle ... a
wide ... arc ... embracing ... a ... closure ... an ...

**(≈ 3 begins moving swiftly over the whole
floor, rhythmically seeing a rope by itself
moving (rope moving to what the text is saying))**

en-   (≈ 3 enacts an "en-circle-ment"—with a "rope" (slowly, carefully))
circle-
ment . . .

        (3 stops in the "en-circle-ment" stance)

if I only had feet   **(1, 2, 4 feet wiggle)**

to claim . . .

Motored Movement

lift arm . . . aim . . . *whap!*   **(≈ 1, 2, 4 lift an arm . . . aim . . . and
slap hand on the floor)**

there's purpose for you . . .

whipped up . . .

unfeeling

minimal show . . .

¿TALK?   **(CLIP (14 sec.) of American Imperialist Forces on the
move (tanks, transport vehicles, infantry, etc.))**

. . .

. . .

you want   **(3, 4 together, side by side, begin walking toward upper-
left stage, diagonally)**

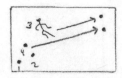

"one"

afterwards? **(3, 4 stop)**

tuck it in   **(clip off)**

---

reel it ... uncoil ... lightly ... swiftly ... bend ... *bend*
        **(≈ 4 begins walking over the stage floor
        seeing a rope doing things that the text says)**

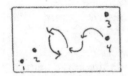

(context ...)   **(quick flash of previous CLIP (2 sec.))**

showering ...   **(• 4 bends into (standing) collapsed stance)**

all over ...

all over ...   **(4 stands and faces the spectators in neutral stance,
        eyes fixed forward)**

all ... under ... stare ...

plastered stare ...

folly

(perfect!)

(perfect)

(in   **(1, 2 begin to roll onto their backs)**

side . . .	**(1, 2 on their backs)**
out)	**(CLIP (8 sec.) of chairs in reverse order: an empty bed, empty chairs around a dining table, empty stadium chairs, empty auditorium chairs)**
(out)	**(5, coming from the spectator area, approaches the players' area swiftly)**

(clip off)

---

there . . . a little loop . . . slipping . . . sliding . . . swerving . . .

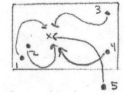

(≈ 5 slows down once on the stage and slowly goes toward the center)

here . . . a slight . . .	**(1-4 rise up and walk toward 5)**
en-circle-ment	**(1-4 gently and carefully encircle 5)**
ffff . . . \<it!\>	**(5 lowers, bending knees / sitting on ankles, and tucks arms around him / her self)**

infinitesimal

I've been here before—

I'm not the same—

I *compose* "power"— **(1–4 wrap arms onto each others shoulders in a tight circle)**

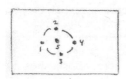

If I only had hands

to claim . . .

touch . . . to . . .

ffff **(1–4 lower down, bending knees / sitting on ankles)**

(sink, baby, sink, sink . . .

tumble . . . seep out . . . swim

into the wider world)

TO BE MASTERFUL **(1–5 still)**

sh-sh-sh . . . *sh* . . . *sh* . . .

reach

reach

reach

reach

END OF BODY MOVEMENT POEM

SPINE

A BODY MOVEMENT POEM FOR THREE PLAYERS

Players: "A" "B" "C" can be of any age, gender, or accent

Objects: a vertical beam (or pole, or pillar, or tree trunk) might already be present in the space; if not, it can be mimed; a table, a fork and knife, a wallet (with bills inside), a notepad

———

{A has hands on the beam, "holding it up" (the beam is about to fall on A). The beam emits heat, so A's hands, feeling great discomfort at holding it up, momentarily lift off the beam (every five seconds or so); at least 30 seconds of this hold-up / touch-off action activity before A speaks}

{A} **It's ... not ... the main ... thing ... this ... it's ... the extensions ... above ... and away ... far ... each ... dangling ... reaching ... vine ... each ... fruit ... emotion ... thought ... sound ... fading ... slightly ... slightly ... expiring ...**

The light!
          Coming down!
                    A waterfall!

I can *see* my hands.

{A continues holding up the beam for 15 seconds}

{A to self, dumbstruck}

**There's no reason *at all*
for these hands
to be
here.**

{A, on "to be / here" unconcernedly lets go of the pillar, gazes at both hands, then walks to the table, lays down on top of it, curls up (facing spectators), head tucked in hands}

{B enters the area, moves in the manner of a person after a long day of labor; sits at the table [fork and knife are on the table], picks up fork (looks at it) then knife (looks at it), then contemptuously claps them together and tosses them on the floor as a workwoman/man might do having been assigned shoddy tools to work with}

{A suddenly springs up on the table (in a sitting position), and in a jerky Pinocchio-like manner—with mechanical intonation}

What sort
of
home entertainment
                                    center
do **you want?**

{B, eyes open wide, grabs at A's hand as at a piece of fried chicken, and struggles to put it in his/her mouth}

{A, shocked/grossed out, after a brief struggle contemptuously withdraws hand, jumps off the table, grabs the fork and knife off the floor, proceeds to the beam, and treats it as a meal, knifing off morsels while glaring at B; A's eyes are wide open, excited, as if saying "yum yum, dumb chum, come get some"}

{B, stilled, glares back, then walks in the direction of A, but then suddenly stops midway when spying something directly above; B then jumps straight up with one arm raised snatching a "fruit"; looks at it –}

{A drops fork and knife when B grasps fruit, then goes back to holding up the beam}

{C comes into the area, swaggering, sidles right up next to B, and says to B (without looking at B, B paying no attention)}

Your old god just died, asshole.

{B tosses fruit away; B then jumps up again and snatches another fruit, looks at it}

{C} **You've *already* sweetly smothered your new god's spirit, *standdown!***

{B tosses fruit away}

{B jumps up again, grabs a branch, grips it, and agonizingly spirals down to the ground as it's breaking; B covers face from falling debris; B's life then "slips away"}

{C walks over, kicks B's body a few times, frisks B's pockets for the wallet [B has wallet with bills inside], finds it, looks inside, counts the cash, then throws the empty wallet at B's body}

{C walks over to A and brandishes the handful of bills in A's face}

{A, spying C holding the wad of cash (and desirous of it), leans face in the direction of cash, but is afraid to let go of the beam. A then suddenly snatches the cash from C's hand, stuffs it into pocket and brusquely props C's two hands on the beam}

{C is shocked; the beam burns C's hands, and C must hold up the beam as A has done}

{A walks over to B, clears the debris from B's body, then drags B below the table; A now sits on the floor, in front of the "TV", fidgeting with "remote control" to get it to work}

{B props up after A has gotten the remote to "work"; B is startled at having awakened in such a strange space, hands motioning as if stuck inside an aquarium; B, in a commercial-like intonation}

Compact, compatible, integratable, portable, versatile, streamlined design, user friendly.

{A is all the while silent, only mildly interested in the "the show"}

{B goes back to anxious stuck-in-aquarium behavior}

{A whips head around to C with angry eyes}

{C responds by wanting to let go of the beam, but being afraid it will fall; C runs out a short distance, stops, looks up, spies a fruit and quickly jumps up to grab it; C then lobs it to A; C immediately returns to the beam to hold it up}

{A catches it, looks at it}

{C blurts out} **Be a *real* human!**

{A "tosses" the fruit at the spectators}

{B is still behaving mystified at being locked inside the aquarium / console / TV / social soul}

{C again lets go of the beam, runs out to grab a fruit, sees it, then lobs it to A; A again glances at it and discards it}

{B} **Intercorporeal adapter pack not included!?**

{B crawls out from under the table, stands firmly, and very markedly says}

I'm a sap for anything that's been, a sieve for anyone, for anything

{B begins stalking the space, sometimes weaving, sometimes prancing in rhythm to the line, repeated over and over; the tone changes with every utterance: at times inquisitive, at times angry, at other times half-mad with joy}

{while B is moving to and fro intoning the line, A springs up and beelines toward C; A knocks over the beam, C flinches, terrified of the falling objects}

{A hurriedly but meticulously kicks away the "fallen objects," making a space to lie down in; A lies down on side, Odalisque-like)}

{C is meanwhile frozen by both A's and B's behavior, confused as to whether to lie down like A, or join in B's madcap dance; C's response it to take out a pocket-sized notepad and begin "writing" furiously (eyes glued to the pad)}

{B, still whirling all over and speaking the line, swooshes by C, grabs the pad, then tosses it to one of the non-players in the space [pad has "Thou shouldst . . . " verses written on it]; B freezes on the toss, arm extended}

110

{A} **Read, read what's there.**

{non-player reads, markedly, measuredly}

"Thou shouldst plant a tree."

**"Thou shouldst eat of the forbidden sweet corn
and put the denuded ear into a small juice-bottle."**

**"Thou shouldst position it between two small limbs of the young
sapling."**

"T'will provide a refreshing respite from flies."

{non-player tosses pad back onto the floor next to A}

{B walks toward the table, gets on top of the table, prostrate, and
proceeds to bodily move as he/she did while intoning "I'm a sap . . ."
line, though silently / unconscious}

{C then walks toward the table and unceremoniously lays on top of it
next to B; C does as B does); 20 seconds pass before A speaks (B and
C keep moving as A speaks)}

{A} **I can't seem to move. From here. Like this. And there's a
tree—oh, there *used to be* a tree! that's blocking out the incoming
darkness behind me.**

{A then slowly rolls over onto stomach and "dies"}

{when B and C hear A's clap on floor, they stop moving, look in the
direction of A, then at each other, then leap off the table and walk
toward A; they kick A to see if "alive or dead," assess A's mass and
volume (as movers would a load they're about to lift), stretch/prep,
agree at angles of lift, then heave-ho A into scarecrow position; A has
eyes closed, is limp, but responds to their doll-formation direction;
B and C spread A's arms out, adjusting as craftwomen/men would a
sculpture; they spread out A's fingers until A's hands look like claws;
B dusts off A's chest for the final "installation," pulls pants' pockets
down for a final primping, steps back, and gestures with hands as if
saying "okay, that's good right about there"}

{as B and C step back to view A, A opens eyes, staring straight ahead, unblinking}

{B} **Holy—Judas—a scarecrow!**

{C flings up both hands skyward (fingers pulled up by sky, toes down by earth, swaying with eyes closed, in a trance}

{B carefully walks C to the table (hands on C's hips) as C is weaving; when they reach the table, B puts both hands on C's shoulders and a foot behind C's knee and gives a slight push to "collapse" C down onto the ground; B then drags C under the table; C moves in a slowly convulsive manner; B starts to walk off the area, when suddenly—}

{A} **Does anyone here have a developed sense of bookspeak?**

{B freezes, turns around, looks at A, goes out to collect wallet (puts it in pocket), collects knife and fork from the ground; B then walks toward A; B carefully/craftily places the fork in one of A's hands (with the same sculptor-like artfulness as before), then the knife in the other hand; B clasps A's hands tight, making sure A's got them in a sure grip; B steps back and does a final sweep of the hand, as if to say "voila"}

{B starts walking back to the table—}

{A} **Does anyone here have a developed sense of bookspeak?**

{if table is light enough to be lifted, C pushes it up in the air when A says "does anyone here . . . "; B looks back at A for a moment, but continues to the table; upon reaching it, B stops, lowers the table (C goes back to convulsions) sits on it, looks inside the wallet, raises it high above the head (making sure there's nothing in it); B then tosses it out to the audience; B then climbs up on the table and lays down, facing up in a casual (cross-legged) Sunday park manner (foot jiggling, relaxed); all players remain in their respective positions for at least 30 seconds.

END OF BODY MOVEMENT POEM

Clock, Deck, and Movement

A MODULAR POETIC ACTIVITIES PIECE FOR FIVE PLAYERS

Players can be of any age, gender, or accent

A rectangular table is set longways right-stage to left-stage. Chairs ("1" & "2") are placed in the following positions (letters correspond to player positions). Players "A," "B," and "C" each have a microphone. Prearranged on the table are A's "Continuous Text" (CT), B & C's "Zero Friends" deck (ZF), and the "Body Movement Parameter" deck (BMP). Players "D" and "E" each have (abridged) copies of the BMP deck in their pockets.

Throughout the piece, each player engages in an "activity" (sometimes alone, sometimes with others). This piece has a total of six activities.

1. A's Continuous Text Activity

A enters into the area of activity, sits at the table, and begins reading the CT at a medium volume. A reads all the way through to the end of the CT text 1. When A finishes reading the last variation of CT text 1 ("spraaawling-over-it-lushness"), finishing with *that's—no fault of mine, man,* A turns the page and begins reading CT text 2. CT1 alternates with CT2 for twenty pages. They are placed on top of a whole ream of unprinted paper.

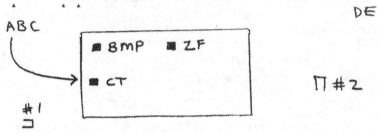

2. D & E's Body Movement Parameters Activity

After A finishes reading the last line of CT text 2 (*"that's—no fault of mine, man"*), D & E come into the area and stand to the far left of the table. D & E both have BMP decks in their pockets (to insure they don't run out of BMPs, both players should have two back-to-back decks). Each deck contains the same lines as the BMP text on the table. However, each card has designation as to which player is going to do a BMP. Also, the decks are interspersed with blank cards, each designated as either a "tosser" or a "placer" (for complete notes to the BMP deck, see "notes to Activity 3").

Simultaneous to A's activity, D & E begin to read their cards (to themselves, not out loud) and then do BMPs. E goes first.

If the card chosen is blank, the player looks at it, considers its blankness, and either tosses it or places it somewhere on the floor. The placing is not done in a matter-of-fact manner, but with great deliberation—ceremonial almost. If the card has a BMP on it, the player reads the card (silently), while (sonically) tuning into to A's activity (later, tuning in to all activities), then moves to the BMP. The other player either studiously looks on or moves to carefully adjust the partner's movement. For example, an arm might be re-positioned at a different angle, or a knee might be simply touched, so that the player in motion lowers it a bit. Also, at times (at every seventh BMP), a player models a different way of doing the BMP, in which case the other pauses their BMP and focuses on the other player's modeling. Each BMP ends in a rather sudden manner, but somewhat gently, and without fanfare. Sometimes the reading and thinking take up as much time as the BMP itself.

In Lab (weeks before the performance), D & E have individually come up with a physically demonstrative "psychic triggering" for each BMP. Neither of them knows the outlines of the other's triggering, whether it originates from some sort of trauma, or dream, or fuzzy memory of some real-life experience. In this way, "adjustments" are live improvised calibrations of two triggering systems. And though the BMPs register the harmonic overtones of the other activities, they must by no means fall into mimesis. Also, D & E's facial gestures remain fluid throughout the whole activity.

The activity ends when the last ZF card has been read in B & C's "Zero Friends" activity (#45 "Zero Friends crawling over craggy bluffs of barren national epics, *for now.*").

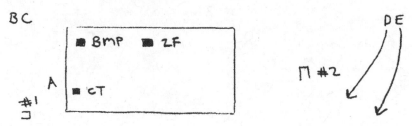

3. B and C's Zero Friends Activity

When A finishes reading CT text 2's last line ("*that's—no fault of mine, man*"), B & C, in a relaxed manner, enter and sit at the table. They take their time settling in. B, at a time of her own choosing, while intently listening to A reading (but not looking at A), picks up a card from the ZF deck. The picking-up is done with great deliberation, never rushing it, as in "should I pick it up now? or wait? . . . okay, here goes." Sometimes the selection is done rather suddenly. Each line from the deck is divided into regular font and *italic* font. B first silently reads the regular-font line, then out loud, then hands C the card. C settles into the moment, gets really close to the mic and reads the "tag" (text in *italic* font). The overall affectation resembles something between an Academy Awards-style presentation (with a bit of suspension between utterances) and a lottery winning-numbers announcement ("and the winner is . . . "). B & C always read at a medium-loud level. B & C alternate picking up cards (and handing them over) all the way to the last card (#45, "Zero Friends crawling over craggy bluffs of barren national epics, *for now*."). Formally speaking, the activity is meant to punctuate A's activity, so a balance has to be struck between creating a steady beat of ZF messages and never rushing B & C's activity. That is to say, B & C's actual (mind & body) attention and readiness is only semi-autonomously related to A's activity.

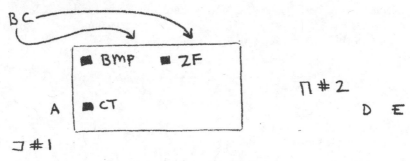

A's adjustment to B & C's activity

When B & C read their ZF cards, A's volume (though not pace) drops considerably, almost to a whisper. When A hears a player read the tag, the sound level rises back up to medium.

4. D, B, and C's New Activity

When the last ZF card is read, "Zero Friends crawling over craggy bluffs of barren national epics, *for now*," A stops reading the CT, and

D & E stop moving to the BMP's. At this point D walks to where A is sitting, A rises from the chair, and D sits. A then walks over to "chair 2" and sits in it. At this point, E walks to "chair 1" and sits in it. Beginning with D, then B, then C (and then back to D and so forth) they each pick a card from the BMP deck and read it. Although they show no hesitation in picking up cards and reading them (into the microphone) their activity is carried out in a decidedly unhurried manner (a minimum of 10 seconds must pass before the next card is picked up and read).

The lines should be read with as little affectation as possible.

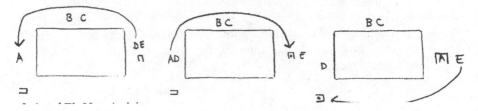

5. A and E's New Activity

Throughout D, B, and C's reading activity, A and E sit in their chairs as they each would at a real-life performance (i.e. a poetry reading). Adjustments of the head, neck, arms, legs, and spine, delineate each players' particular, idiosyncratic way of sitting. In the main, however, they are sitting still.

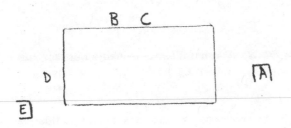

6. All Players New Activity

After the last BMP card is read (#43, "ears detach and take flight in different directions, now"), all players remain still and silent for at least 30 seconds. E then gets up from her/his chair and carries it over to where A is sitting. A gets up from chair #2, and E fits chair #1 on top of #2, so that they're "flush," one chair atop the other. They both then look at their "accomplishment," briefly, but intently, then look at each other and walk off the stage in different directions. D, B, and C then carefully, and ceremoniously, remove the mics, texts, and cards from the table and proceed to turn the table on its back. They look at their "accomplishment", and then at one another, then D & B begin pulling the table toward stage left, but C stops their action (D & B relenting) and drags it back into place. They all look once more at one another, briefly, but intently, and then walk off the stage in the same direction.

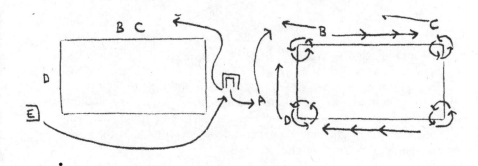

Notes to Activity 1

In the first round of the CT, "A" must clearly delineate between the different imbedded voicings in each CT paragraph, adjusting tone, timbre, but most of all, affect. So that, for example, the stanza . . .

keenness, to keenness, by keenness, as keenness, keenness this of . . . *dot,* 1, siege . . . crawling a stumble to waddle a strutting to prance: it's like i—like, *could* like—*not* liking it, "it's nobody's fault we don't live in radical times", *it's your fault, man*

becomes:

[in a brisk but analytical way, as if proposing a complex mathematical formula] keenness, to keenness, by keenness, as keenness, keenness this of

[in an abrupt, artificial machine-like voice] *dot,* 1, siege

[in a matter-of-fact way, as if what's being described is a normal day's activity] crawling a stumble to waddle a strutting to prance

[imitative of a teenager who's on a cell phone, rising intonation toward the end of the line] it's like i—like, *could* like—*not* liking it

[in a medium pitch, as if in the middle of a spirited discussion among political policy wonks on TV] "it's nobody's fault we don't live in radical times"

[in a somewhat scolding manner, not nasty, but as if coming from a friend, firm, in a lower pitch than the previous line] *it's your fault, man*

Once the piece is well into motion (after several CT pages), A is at liberty to pronounce words and phrases with variating intensities and affects, according to what A is actually feeling about the CT.

Notes to Activity 2

It is important that B & C remain nonplussed by A's kinetic shifts in reading. Though they are reading / appealing somewhat directly to the spectators, they do not acknowledge the spectators with looks or responses. Also, B & C do not look at each other's faces, nor show much familiarity with each other. But at the same time, they are comfortable (though not too loose) with each other throughout the activity.

Notes to Activity 3

For exact BMP card-deck order and designations, see "Body Movement Parameters card-deck designations" text.

D & E should also be familiar with all of the lines of the Zero Friends deck, so that when they hear the first few words of a ZF line, they can (physically or mentally) include the phenomenon into their BMPs.

D & E should not pander to the spectators by placing their bodies in the most obviously (stage front) visible positions. However, the players should keep in mind that the "adjustments" are meant as much for the spectators as for themselves.

Notes to D, B, and C's New Activity (4)

This activity is in essence an appeal to the spectators to not lose themselves in their heads, so "milking it," *lengthening* its delivery (hence its effect) is very important. It must not be rushed in any way.

Notes to Activity 5

A & E's faces must not be stiff, but remain pliable. Eyes must remain alert, lips at the ready.

Notes to Activity 6

All players' actions must be done in a "concerted" manner, that is to say, not casually. Fluidity and crispness of action is required of every effort.

Continuous Text (CT) 1

keenness, to keenness, by keenness, as keenness, keenness this of . . . *dot,* 1, siege . . . crawling a stumble to waddle a strutting to prance: it's like i—like, *could* like—*not* liking it, "it's nobody's fault we don't live in radical times," *it's your fault, man*

limberness, to limberness, by limberness, as limberness, limberness this of . . . *dot,* 2, siege / counter-siege . . . running a stand to jump a landing to tumble: it's like i—like, *could* like—*not* liking it, "it's everybody's fault we don't live in radical times," *it's not my fault, man*

sprightliness, to sprightliness, by sprightliness, as sprightliness, sprightliness this of . . . *dot,* 3, siege / counter-siege / siege . . . pacing a stoop to stand a stilling to surge: it's like i—like, *could* like—*not* liking it, "it's my fault we don't live in radical times," *it's their fault, man*

poking-about-ness, to poking-about-ness, by poking-about-ness, as poking-about-ness, poking-about-ness this of . . . *dot,* 4, siege / counter-siege / siege / counter-siege . . . skidding a slide to smup a streaking to smip: it's like i—like, *could* like—*not* liking it, "it's your fault we don't live in radical times," *it's nobody's fault, man*

stuck-tight-in-the-tautness, to stuck-tight-in-the-tautness, by stuck-tight-in-the-tautness, as stuck-tight-in-the-tautness, stuck-tight-in-the-tautness this of . . . *dot,* 5, siege / counter-siege / siege / counter-siege / siege . . . straggling a jumble to crumble a struggling to strooge: it's like i—like, *could* like—*not* liking it, "it's our fault we don't live in radical times," *it's everybody's fault, man*

jerking-it-around-to-see-what-it-knows-and-what-it-can-really-do-ness, to jerking-it-around-to-see-what-it-knows-and-what-it-can-really-do-ness, by jerking-it-around-to-see-what-it-knows-and-what-it-can-really-do-ness, as jerking-it-around-to-see-what-it-knows-and-what-it-can-really-do-ness, jerking-it-around-to-see-what-it-knows-and-what-it-can-really-do-ness this of . . . *dot,* 6, siege / counter-siege / siege / counter-siege / siege / counter-siege . . . spipping a freeze to frizz a spupping to grot grot grot: it's like i—like, *could* like—*not* liking it, "it's their fault we don't live in radical times," *it's actually, our fault, man*

spraaawling·over·it·lushness, to spraaawling·over·it·lushness, by spraaawling·over·it·lushness, as spraaawling·over·it·lushness, spraaawling·over·it·lushness this of . . . *dot,* 7, siege / counter· siege / siege / counter·siege / siege / counter·siege / siege . . . swooping a suave to strip a skulling to scrap: it's like i—like, *could* like—*not* liking it, "it's my fault we don't live in radical times," *that's—no fault of mine, man*

Continuous Text (CT) 2

numbness, to numbness, by numbness, as numbness, numbness this of . . . *star,* 1, kiss . . . crawling a stumble to waddle a strutting to prance: it's not like i—like, *can't* get to like it, "it's off no one's rump we're not shifting," *it's off yours, man*

soreness, to soreness, by soreness, as soreness, soreness this of . . . *star,* 2, kiss / jolly slap . . . *running* a stand to jump a landing to tumble: it's not like i—like, *can't* get to like it, "it's off everyone's rump we're not shifting," *it's not off mine, man*

stiffness, to stiffness, by stiffness, as stiffness, stiffness this of . . . *star,* 3, kiss / jolly slap / kiss . . . pacing a stoop to stand a stilling to surge: it's not like i—like, *can't* get to like it, "it's off *my* rump we're not shifting," *it's off theirs, man*

crackling·about·ness, to crackling·about·ness, by crackling·about· ness, as crackling·about·ness, crackling·about·ness this of . . . *star,* 4, kiss / jolly slap / kiss / jolly slap . . . skidding a slide to smup a streaking to smip: it's not like i—like, *can't* get to like it, "it's off *your* rump we're not shifting," *it's off no one's, man*

slackening·the·mind·ness, to slackening·the·mind·ness, by slackening·the·mind·ness, as slackening·the·mind·ness, slackening· the·mind·ness this of . . . *star,* 5, kiss / jolly slap / kiss / jolly slap / kiss . . . straggling a jumble to crumble a struggling to strooge: it's not like i—like, *can't* get to like it, "it's off *our* rump we're not shifting," *it's off everyone's, man* knotting·it·up·out·of·no·clue·as·to·how·to·let·her·rip·clean·off·ness, to knotting·it·up·out·of·no·clue·as·to·how·to·let·her·rip·clean·off· ness, by knotting·it·up·out·of·no·clue·as·to·how·to·let·her·rip·clean· off·ness, as knotting·it·up·out·of·no·clue·as·to·how·to·let·her·rip· clean·off·ness, knotting·it·up·out·of·no·clue·as·to·how·to·let·her· rip·clean·off·ness this of ... *star,* 6, kiss / jolly slap / kiss / jolly slap / kiss / jolly slap ... spipping a freeze to frizz a spupping to grot grot grot: it's not like i—like, *can't* get to like it, "it's off *their* rump we're not shifting," *it's actually, off ours, man*

snuggling·under·it·mmmm·ness, to snuggling·under·it·mmmm· ness, by snuggling·under·it·mmmm·ness, as snuggling·under·it· mmmm·ness, snuggling·under·it·mmmm·ness this of ... *star,* 7, kiss / jolly slap / kiss / jolly slap / kiss / jolly slap / kiss ... swooping a suave to strip a skulling to scrap: it's not like i—like, *can't* get to like it, "it's off *my* rump we're not shifting," *that's—asinine, man*

Zero Friends (ZF) card deck

From top of the deck to bottom of the deck

•

Zero Friends quits Zero Friends steering committee, *again.*

Zero Friends insists on nickels and dimes restitution, *for now.*

Zero Friends in emergency room scribbling a pretty darn good "me- me" poem, *again.*

Zero Friends joins provisional Infinite Friends government, *for now.*

Zero Friends forgets the name of crucial latest imaging software, *again.*

Zero Friends locking horns with Zero Friends over Infinite Friends issues, *again.*

Zero Friends with 30% rent increase forgets the name of class-scrambling peripheral hardware device, *ubu booboo.*

Zero Friends visits Zero Friends country, buys Zero Friends agit-prop t-shirt, never wears it—*never?*

Zero Friends don't let Zero Friends make Infinite Friends—*ever?*

Zero Friends on mountaintop about to dry-hump Zero Friends commemorative statue, *again.*

Zero Friends scampering over hot spurts of found environments, *for now.*

Zero Friends *Minoans* somehow, leaping naked over lacquered charging bulls, *again.*

Zero Friends rejoins Zero Friends steering committee, *for now.*

Zero Friends, after some thought, outrageous behavior, more thought, more outrageous behavior, writes a pretty darn good "me-you" poem, *again?*

Zero Friends after a three-year skid hitting Zero Friends circuit hard can't anymore without streamlets for all debts, public and private, *boo hoo hoo.*

Zero Friends gets pennies-from-heaven restitution, *again.*

Zero Friends on a surgery table remembering a pretty darn good "us-versus-them" poem, *again.*

Zero Friends don't let Zero Friends shuck Zero Friends, *ever?*

Zero Friends in alpine depression about to wet hump Infinite Friends lost environment, *again.*

Zero Friends skimming over bushy hillocks of belabored lyrics, *for now.*

Zero Friends *Olmecs* somehow, hefty thoughts sittin' pretty in the sun, *again.*

Zero Friends causing fissures in Zero Friends steering committee, *for now.*

Zero Friends, after some rain, outrageous sun, more rain, more outrageous sun, hardens into a pretty darn good "only-you" poem, *again.*

Zero Friends after a three-year streak hitting Zero Friends circuit hard can't anymore with tin-plated teeth, public and private, *boo-yeah!*

Zero Friends hardwires the name of Infinite Friends foundation tax I.D. number, *boo-yeah!*

Zero Friends under CT scan for 2 hours mumbles a pretty darn good "no-you" poem, *pour toi.*

Zero Friends don't let Infinite Friends steer leaping naked heavenly belabored lyrics—*ever?*

Zero Friends *Etruscans* somehow, happy-wicked marbled smiles—to stroke—*again!?*

Zero Friends wearing out the surface manners of the breakaway splitter steering committee, *again.*

Zero Friends helicoptered into volcano caldera about to blast favorite mp3 clip, *for now.*

Zero Friends, after some lava splatter, overstated chill, more lava splatter, more overstated chill, conceives of a pretty darn good "me-versus-me" poem, *for now.*

Zero Friends phishes access code to Infinite Friends unlimited skull viewing, *again.*

Zero Friends insists on Euros—in hand, *danke.*

Zero Friends stomps over ice-packs of autonomous art environments, *oops.*

Zero Friends reconstitutes New United International Infinite Zero Friends committee, *again.*

Zero Friends sneaks into Zero Friends country, builds Infinite Friends revolutionary ghost theatre, never pimps it—*uh . . . well.*

. Zero Friends don't let Zero Friends cop Infinite Friends—*uh . . . hm.*

Zero Friends on a dry lakebed about to make Infinite Friends backstroke a "no-it" poetics, *again.*

Zero Friends gimping towards cool springs of True-Glam-Trash environments, *for now.*

Zero Friends *Roanokeans* somehow, over-attired stumbling over rotted squash squishing out the seeds of "make it new," *again.*

Zero Friends, after some bleu de lyons, fabulous casino pink, more bleu de lyons, more fabulous casino pink, belts out a pretty darn good "us-v.ersus-us" poem, *again?*

Zero Friends after a three-year cruise hitting Zero Friends circuit hard can't anymore without candy canes for all monsters, public and private, *well—fuck—me.*

Zero Friends accepts pinto beans praise from hellish institution, *again.*

Zero Friends in head-and-neck halo bracing for a pretty darn good "mega-millions me" poem, *again.*

Zero Friends crawling over craggy bluffs of barren national epics, *for now.*

Body Movement Parameters (BMP) deck for player's B, C, & D

From top of the deck to bottom of the deck

1. palms slowly waking up
2. heels gently waking up
3. belly just waking, cranky
4. groin now awake, tingly
5. mid-upper back tensing, still drowsy
6. knees startled into readiness
7. shoulders sensitive to rhythms all around
8. forearm filling up with blood
9. ribcage expanding
10. lower torso lowering and rising at the same time
11. toes twitching, eyelids feeling it
12. thigh commanding whole body to be alert
13. temples waking up, neck tilts backwards in sympathy
14. jawbone loosening, finding its place in the skull
15. buttocks flexing, lips resolute
16. right side of torso wanting to rotate 180 degrees
17. left side of torso wanting to rotate 180 degrees
18. fingers 3-4-5 of left hand pulled by six different regions of the local galaxy cluster
19. left fist being tugged by forces emanating from the ground directly below

20.   inside of elbow asserting its abilities
21.   thumb being pulled by passing clouds
22.   adams apple super-exposed to the unknown ahead
23.   ten toes each wanting to dance to their own rhythm
24.   triceps urging on triceps
25.   index fingers calling forth hamstrings' abilities with
       help of eyes
26.   lower spine alerts upper spine of drooping head
27.   left side of neck induces right calf into a moving stillness
28.   entire front side of the body makes its presence known to
       entire back side of the body
29.   upper side of wrists speak their abilities to forehead eager
       to listen
30.   back of head reeling in scalp, nostrils opening
31.   left middle finger hearing a rush of urine redirected
       through left arm via right kidney of someone in the room
32.   right knee begins to breathe—finally
33.   tips of all ten fingers play-acting as ten stomachs
       contracting hungry but with no clear memory of food
34.   lungs lead top of the skull into polka-punk rhythm
35.   inside lining of stomach wills two outstretched invisible
       arms to embrace everyone in the room
36.   tongue and arch of foot agitated over lower groin's sudden
       contraction
37.   whole front of the body takes flight on its own with its own
       conception of "what's out there"
38.   back of the palms drawn to kidneys, kidneys aloof
39.   eyeballs retreating into skull for a refreshing swim in the
       lungs
40.   shoulder socket shocks pinky into heated struggle over
       who-the-hell-knows-what
41.   back of throat wakes up (peacefully)
42.   inner thighs struggle against dozing off
43.   ears detach and take flight in different directions, now

Body Movement Parameters (BMP) card deck designations for players D & E

From top of the deck to bottom of the deck

Showing alternations between players.

Bold letters indicate that the other player does a BMP adjustment, i.e., "(E) **(D)**" means that when E does a movement, D adjusts it.

(t) "tosser" card
(p) "placer" card

•

1. palms slowly waking up (E)

2. (t) **(E)**

3. heels gently waking up (E)

4. belly just waking, cranky (E) **(D)**

5. groin now awake, tingly (D)

6. mid-upper back tensing, still drowsy (E)

7. (p) (D)

8. knees startled into readiness (D)

9. shoulders sensitive to rhythms all around (D)

10. forearm filling up with blood (D)

11. ribcage expanding (E) **(D)**

12. lower torso lowering and rising at the same time (D)

13. toes twitching, eyelids feeling it (D)

14. thigh commanding whole body to be alert (E)

15. temples waking up, neck tilts backwards in sympathy (D)

16. (t) **(D)**

17. jawbone loosening, finding its place in the skull (D)

18. buttocks flexing, lips resolute (D) **(E)**

19. right side of torso wanting to rotate 180 degrees (E)

20. left side of torso wanting to rotate 180 degrees (D)

21. (p) (E)

22. fingers 3-4-5 of both hands pulled by six different regions of the local galaxy cluster **(E)**

23. left fist being tugged by forces emanating from the ground directly below (E)

24. inside of elbow asserting its abilities (E)

25. thumb being pulled by passing clouds (D) **(E)**

26. Adam's apple super-exposed to the unknown ahead (E)

27. ten toes each wanting to dance to its own rhythm (E)

28. triceps urging on triceps (D)

29. index fingers calling forth hamstrings' abilities with help of eyes (E)

30. (t) (E)

31. lower spine alerts upper spine of drooping head (E)

32. left side of neck induces right calf into a moving stillness (E)
(D)

33. entire front side of the body makes its presence known to entire back side of the body (D)

34. upper side of wrists speak their abilities to forehead eager to listen (E)

35. (p) (D)

36. back of head reeling in scalp, nostrils opening (D)

37. left middle finger hearing a rush of urine redirected through left arm via right kidney of someone in the room (D)

38. right knee begins to breathe—finally (D)

39. tips of all ten fingers play-acting as ten stomachs contracting hungry but with no clear memory of food (E) **(D)**

40. lungs lead top of the skull into polka-punk rhythm (D)

41. inside lining of stomach wills two outstretched invisible arms to embrace everyone in the room (D)

42. tongue and arch of foot agitated over lower groin's sudden contraction (E)

43. whole front of the body takes flight on its own with its own conception of "what's out there" (D)

44. (t) (D)

45. back of the palms drawn to kidneys, kidneys aloof (D)

46. eyeballs retreating into skull for a refreshing swim in the lungs (D) **(E)**

47. shoulder socket shocks pinky into heated struggle over who-the-hell-knows-what (E)

48. back of throat wakes up (peacefully) (D)

49. (p) (E)

50. inner thighs struggle against dozing off (E)

51. ears detach and take flight in different directions, now (E)

END OF MODULAR POETIC ACTIVITIES PIECE

MEMORIES OF SOMEWHERE, TO SOMEWHERE ELSE

A POETICS TRIALOGUE

VOICES: regular font, *italic,* and **bold**

—

When not in shuffle mode you know what I mean, *shuffle?*
(poly wants a monad wants to compre-squawk what's meant by—)

When not pinned-down on "selective" "moments"
pervy screen—sticky—the news the screws the flooze of—

When not in elevated baby-chair, bare-faced spanked-up ugly in
the—

Whoa . . . that's bangin' around in your head! not mine . . .

But you know . . . what's on is on . . . pro-ceed, my friend

The now

The now?

Spanked up—ugly—in the now

*That I can see. But what's this "when not" business? "When not" this
that, the other . . . mere suspense? a blind spot in some story?*

Signs, obviously . . . configuring some kinda social logic, the
outlines of a temporality . . . as yet unspoken. At any rate, they're
not things in my head . . . of that I assure you. I mean "I" ain't no
guarantor of anything.

*Yeah yeah I gotcha there, but, what exactly . . . uh . . . well . . . maybe it's
best you just do your thing for now . . . flow on through . . . spin this space
a while*

Spin I do, spin I must. But maybe you can kick-in with something
too . . . perhaps together we can conjure up a volatile space . . .
where signs shake off their "natural selves" . . . cloak and de-cloak,
you know?

*Yeah, okay, all right . . . But aren't signs already doing that—in the
world? World of necessity, world of necessity's expression . . . apart from
any "special" conjuring?*

Of course, yes, so this "conjuring" . . . it's bestriding all that.

*I hear you . . . you mean like . . . epistantagonal suppositings poly-
looping materially mundus in superstrings—relations—matters of
matters—tying knots, cutting ribbons, tresses . . .*

Uhhh . . . *right.* How 'bout you repeat this "when *not* in shuffle / when
not in shuffle" stuff maybe like five or six times . . . but each time,
shave off a syllable. That way memory (somatic-semantic memory)
can tie up some of the slack. You say the string and I'll be inserting
a sort of lyric in there, ready?

Uh huh . . .

when not in shuffle—
    Living, they say, is
when not in shuff—
    For simplicities sake, or
when not in—
    For complexities sake, or
when not—
    For the sake of nothing, or
when—
    For the sake of something
s p e c i a l

Or that life itself is cavalierish enough to—
    They? never really say—

But what do *you* say?

Bubble in the chicken soup of what's said . . .

Umbrage of let's paddle though the rudder's jammed . . .

Whoa . . . That's pretty poetic there.

Actually not. Not by some standards.

Yeah, I hear that, "standards" . . .

Anyway, I'm starting to wonder myself what this "shuffle" thing's all about . . .

Well, maybe we can re- . . . volatize that somehow . . .

I like that, "re-volitalize" . . .   But how?

Well I've got these notes here, actually . . .

—Oh good, good—shoot!

. . . though . . . not sure if it's shuffle itself, or a break in shuffle . . . but here goes . . .

Photogenic / Compliant

Lemon soldiers, expression
Spontaneous gaieties
Gone sour

Bunkered down among
News sessions, speakable
Heads, spherical
Squeezlings, the levitates
Squirt outs

Tag touchers
Rippers

They squeeze their end-points
The whole other story is of by smearing it

Odd jovial
Mogul-like moan under a stone
Mossy

Monadic

Splinterable

Ethic

Shrill summer's a' comin' in—goin' goin'—blank—cope—
Shrill summer's a' comin' in—goin' goin'—blank—cope—

And the thing is still
seared in this—

what should we call it—
"brain?"

phew! . . . That's *gotta be* a poem . . . (by-some-standard)

Yeah, yeah, but what do you think? You think we're hittin' on the same
thing?

Hell I don't know . . . but let's . . . or I'm thinking . . . didn't you say

"Bunkered down . . . among
sessions"

didn't you say

· "speakable
heads,

the levitates"
Weird that—or something like that
free-floating

(like Capital *ain't* "free,"
but forced, so *flipped over* as—"free")

also something about

"Shrill summer's a' comin' in—goin' goin'—blank—cope—"

"blank—cope"

and something about

"brain"

should we call it that

*Man . . . you're sounding like that polly-wants-a-monad—and quick!
Hey, why don't we trick it up some . . . to see if it's the* stuff *of shuffle . . .
or some kinda* anti-shuffle . . .

Alright, I'm game . . . (Some way to spend the day, huh? I can hear
my mother now . . . "Que es eso . . . un . . . *hohbee?* . . . o? . . . ")

*Listen, listen . . . why don't we smush that sequence we did before with
some of that . . . my uh . . . so-called poem there . . .*

Really? . . .   That's gonna be one fat lentil burger . . .

*Uh huh . . . I'm also wondering if we should fling in the actual sign
'shuffle' . . . like whenever, you know—fidgety . . . but maybe under the
cover of something . . . like . . . ka'-flinga-bling-bling . . . (ka'-flinga-bling-
bling . . . Ah yeeah . . . "hohbee")*

Alright alright . . . that'll work . . .   Let's take a fiver . . . maybe bring
Dick and Jane into it, then run it . . .

   . . .
   . . .

when not in shuffle **[Photogenic / Compliant]**

  Living, they say, is

when not in [Lemon soldiers, expression] shuff—

For simplicities sake, or

when not in— **[Gone sour / Bunkered down among]**

For complexities sake **[sessions]**, or

when not—

For the sake of <ka'·flinga·bling·bling> nothing, or <ka'·flinga·bling·bling>

[speakable / Heads]

when—

For the sake of something **[spherical / Squeezlings, the levitates]**

s p e c i a l

[Squirt outs]

Or that <ka'·flinga·bling·bling> life itself is cavalierish enough to

—they **[The whole other story is of by smearing it]** never really say—

But what do *you* **[Shrill summer's a' comin' in—goin' goin'— blank—cope—]** say?

Bubble in the chicken soup of what's <ka'·flinga·bling·bling> said .
. .

Umbrage of **[what should we call it]** let's paddle though the rudder's **["brain?"]** jammed . . . "

. . . um . . . just keep going . . . say what's left

Tag touchers
Rippers

They squeeze their end-points

Odd jovial
Mogul-like moan under a stone
Mossy

Monadic

Splinterable

And the thing is still

seared in this . . .

Together now:

WHAT SHOULD WE CALL IT—

"BRAIN"?

. . .
. . .

Hey, you know what? . . . That makes *no sense* whatsoever . . .

and somehow . . . it makes *more* sense too . . .

by-some-standards!

By Some Standards

. . .
. . .

Did you see that couple looking at us through the window?

Who? I didn't see anybody . . . oh, you mean that billboard across the street?

Yeah, that one with the waterfall, the power jeep, the ferns at attention bowing . . . you think *they're* the squeezers of those nozzles of those hoses of those pumps . . . so prim & primed?

You know what, let's bag this for now—what do you say?

Yeah, okay, let's *bounce* on outta here (*not* shuffle)

Yeah—not shuffle

To somewhere else.

END OF TRIALOGUE

GREAT AWAKENING

A MINIMALLY STAGED DIALOGUE FOR TWO PLAYERS

{B being pulled over by cop, nervous, skittish; A "cop" walks up from behind wearing shades, aggressive, zealous, knocks on the "window"}

A: The lord can—give you a will, for the right search.

B: I twitch, jerk, and quake—as a prime example—of that search.

A: The lord looks for prime examples.

B: The lord is hereby offered one.

A: Self-recognition, the cognate in common?

B: We've got an understanding—me, you, the lord.

A: Weep not says the lord, for—

B: —a well-lent will, can more easily skim, him?

A: The lord's cognition has spoken.

B: The lord seeks exactness?

{A pulls B from car and puts B's hands on the hood}

A: Awake—from yourself. Shark-teaser in a cage—have exactitude!

B: The lord twitches, jerks, and quakes—I didn't think so, until now.

A: I offer myself, as proof.

B: People from cities all over, unable to analyze it—guilt-free, come to—

A: —fight? Amen!

B: Amen.

A: The lord, the pimp, the people, the product, the pump of this culture readied (a stainless-steel ring to pull in an emergency)

B: Amen.

A: A platinum collar, cold on contact, sometimes bliss, around the neck.

B: Pull, then twist, so that the hidden holiday is revealed: Katrina Day.

A: The food pantry of X the Lord's Sanctuary—*is* inviting.

B: Chew on this, profit.

A: Nylon straps, snug as the lord's words tethering the lord's—

B: Independent Contracting Schemes (a toddler seat at the table)

{A muscles B to the ground into spread-eagle position}

A: Amen. Let's be exact! There's art for profits, art for *non*-profits (to profit by), and altogether *unprofitable* arts.

B: Quantum. Sociology. My fifty golden calves—at granny hipster's.

A: A small slab of anthracite for the nephew, an ornate cape—just for the hell of it, a hockey mask for a stroll through the mall, a 500 megawatt pulsed rhodamine laser in hand—etc.

B: You. Proud product of some kind of network. I think the lord's *self-pimping* abilities—are on the increase.

A: Average poetry readings reveal much.

B: I improve . . . when the content is based on *some other kind of*—contract.

A: Respect for The Lord! Respect for Cable Coppersmooth, Cinnamon Face, and all verifiable accomplishments, in tow.

B: The local is pushed out. Amen?

A: Amen! This re-flavoring of certain . . . distinctions. Other bitterness' applied lightly to the rippled surface. Property mud bars for the whole family!

B: Audit the flow—*incoming. Admit* the lord. You were about to This Very Moaning In Private Seems Necessary. What's the immediate effect?

A: Piety, double-digit snide, "bilk bilk."

B: What's the immediate goal?

A: Light up the mall.

B: And the lonely shark around the cage?

A: Amen. The people *are*—poking back—at it.

END OF DIALOGUE

THE MAKINGS

A PRELUDE TO A NIGHT OF POETICS THEATER PERFORMANCES

Players {A, B, C, D}

Positions: A, northwest; B, northeast; C, southwest; D, southeast

{players enter the center space as they speak their first lines;
players end up in a (horizontal) line for the remainder of the piece}

{A}   Living in your own thunder.

        Seeking a connection.

        Framing the spillage.

        Lunging, plunging.

{B}   Heavy heavy.

{C}   Dust moat, afloat.

{D}   Fiery gnat!

{C}   Spasticus Elasticus.

{B}   Saint.

{C}   Let's light up a saint!

{B}   Smoke! {coughs}

{D}   Charred, *too* charred—hold open that bag . . . *here* you go.

{A} {steps toward the spectators}

> It's never alright.
>
> It's never, never alright
>
> To be a poet
>
> A living poet.
>
> And the pillars remain in place, and the pillars come piling down.
>
> And there's dust.
>
> And coughing and sneezing and wheezing.

{A heads back to the line}

> And it all gets washed out—in water—*wet* water.
>
> And it all dries up—hardens—to rock.
> Plain combustible carbon.

{A, B, C, D}

> ¡EGO!

{A}   And it *crrracks.*

> Like this (*crrrrr*) like this (*crrrrr*) like this (*crrrrr*)

{B}   Practically mindless, this mess.

{C}   Psychically useful, mass muttering?

{A}   It's all right.

        It's *gotta be* all right.

        Burn kindle in the cavern.

        It's thundering outside.

{A, B, C, D}

        WHO'S STILL IN THE CAVERN—STAY!

{B}

        Though it's only poetic theater's faux duress,

        It's a vantage point, nonetheless.

POETICS THEATER is a test of poetry. The Collapsible Poetics Theater is an all volunteer effort, one that assembles itself within a given 24-72 hour period of each performance. Each locale (with its resident poets, experienced actors, experienced non-actors) brings an entirely new set of possibilities. It is reminiscent of Commedia Dell'Arte in its traveling, portable, rapid-set-up qualities. Poetics Theater fits into the poetry scene as a baby does in itchy burlap; it fits into the drama scene as does a little crown, little scepter, little gown, all neatly stored in a metal suitcase (quite literally). The dings are just dings.

RODRIGO TOSCANO is the author of *To Leveling Swerve, Platform, The Disparities,* and *Partisans.* His poetry has appeared in *Best American Poetry 2004, War and Peace* (2004 & 2007), and in *The Criminal's Cabinet: An anthology of poetry and fiction* (2004), and in *McSweeney's Poets Picking Poets.* He was a 2005 recipient of a New York State Fellowship in Poetry. Toscano is the writer and artistic coordinator for the Collapsible Poetics Theater (CPT). His polyvocalic pieces, poetics plays, and body-movement poems have been performed at the Disney Redcat Theater in Los Angeles, Ontological-Hysteric Poet's Theater Festival, Poet's Theater Jamboree 2007, and the Yockadot Poetics Theater Festival. His radio pieces have appeared on WPIX FM (New York), KAOS Public Radio Olympia, WNYU, and PS.1 Radio. His work has been translated into French, German, Italian, and Catalonian. Toscano is originally from Southern California. He works in Manhattan at the Labor Institute, and lives in Brooklyn.

FENCE BOOKS is an extension of *Fence,* a biannual journal of poetry, fiction, art, and criticism that has a mission to redefine the terms of accessibility by publishing challenging writing distinguished by idiosyncrasy and intelligence rather than by allegiance with camps, schools, or cliques. It is part of our press's mission to support writers who might otherwise have difficulty being recognized because their work doesn't answer to either the mainstream or to recognizable modes of experimentation.

Since 2008 Fence Books has been a participating publisher in the National Poetry Series.

The Motherwell Prize (formerly the Alberta Prize) is an annual series that offers publication of a first or second book of poems by a woman, as well as a one thousand dollar cash prize.

Our third prize series is the Fence Modern Poets Series. This contest is open to poets of any gender and at any stage of career, and offers a one thousand dollar cash prize in addition to book publication.

For more information about the National Poetry Series, visit www.nationalpoetryseries.org.

For more information about our other prizes, visit www.fenceportal.org, or send an SASE to: Fence Books/[Name of Prize], New Library 320, University at Albany, 1400 Washington Avenue, Albany, NY, 12222.

For more about Fence, visit www.fenceportal.org.

Fence Books

THE MOTHERWELL PRIZE

Aim Straight at the Fountain and Press Vaporize	Elizabeth Marie Young
Unspoiled Air	Kaisa Ullsvik Miller

THE ALBERTA PRIZE

The Cow	Ariana Reines
Practice, Restraint	Laura Sims
A Magic Book	Sasha Steensen
Sky Girl	Rosemary Griggs
The Real Moon of Poetry and Other Poems	Tina Brown Celona
Zirconia	Chelsey Minnis

FENCE MODERN POETS SERIES

Star in the Eye	James Shea
Structure of the Embryonic Rat Brain	Christopher Janke
The Stupefying Flashbulbs	Daniel Brenner
Povel	Geraldine Kim
The Opening Question	Prageeta Sharma
Apprehend	Elizabeth Robinson
The Red Bird	Joyelle McSweeney

NATIONAL POETRY SERIES

Collapsible Poetics Theater	Rodrigo Toscano

ANTHOLOGIES & CRITICAL WORKS

*Not for Mothers Only: Contemporary Poets on Child-Getting &
Child-Rearing*   Catherine Wagner & Rebecca Wolff, editors

POETRY

The Method	Sasha Steensen
The Orphan & Its Relations	Elizabeth Robinson
Site Acquisition	Brian Young
Rogue Hemlocks	Carl Martin
19 Names for Our Band	Jibade Khalil Huffman
Infamous Landscapes	Prageeta Sharma
Bad Bad	Chelsey Minnis
Snip Snip!	Tina Brown Celona
Yes, Master	Michael Earl Craig
Swallows	Martin Corless-Smith
Folding Ruler Star	Aaron Kunin
The Commandrine & Other Poems	Joyelle McSweeney
Macular Hole	Catherine Wagner
Nota	Martin Corless-Smith
Father of Noise	Anthony McCann
Can You Relax in My House	Michael Earl Craig
Miss America	Catherine Wagner

FICTION

Flet: A Novel	Joyelle McSweeney
The Mandarin	Aaron Kunin